Contents

ARTHUR MILLER

Death of a Salesman

with commentary and notes by
ENOCH BRATER

Series Editor: Enoch Brater

ANDOVER COLLEGE

Bloomsbury Methuen Drama
An imprint of Bloomsbury Publishing Plc

B L O O M S B U R Y
LONDON · OXFORD · NEW YORK · NEW DELHI · SYDNEY

Bloomsbury Methuen Drama
An imprint of Bloomsbury Publishing Plc

Imprint previously known as Methuen Drama

50 Bedford Square	1385 Broadway
London	New York
WC1B 3DP	NY 10018
UK	USA

www.bloomsbury.com

**BLOOMSBURY, METHUEN DRAMA and
the Diana logo are trademarks of Bloomsbury Publishing Plc**

This edition first published 2010
Reprinted 2010, 2011, 2012, 2013 (three times), 2015, 2016, 2017

British Library Cataloguing-in-Publication Data
A catalogue record for this book is available from the British Library.

ISBN: PB: 978-1-4081-0841-3
ePDF: 978-1-4742-2557-1
ePUB: 978-1-4742-2556-4

Library of Congress Cataloging-in-Publication Data
A catalog record for this book is available from the Library of Congress.

Series: Student Editions

Printed and bound in India

Arthur Miller: 1915–2005

1915   17 October: Arthur Asher Miller born in New York City, the second of Isidore (Izzy) and Augusta (Gussie) Barnett Miller's three children. His brother Kermit born in 1912, sister Joan 1922.

1920–   Attends PS 24 in Harlem, then an upper-middle-
28   class Jewish neighbourhood, where his mother went to the same school. The family lives in an apartment overlooking Central Park on the top floor of a six-storey building at 45 West 110th Street, between Lenox and Fifth Avenues. Takes piano lessons, goes to Hebrew school and ice-skates in the park. His Barnett grandparents are nearby on West 118th Street. In summers the extended family rents a bungalow in Far Rockaway. Sees his first play in 1923, a melodrama at the Schubert Theatre.

1928   His father's successful manufacturing business in the Garment District, the Miltex Coat and Suit Company, with as many as 800 workers, begins to see hard times faced with the looming Depression. The family moves from Manhattan to rural Brooklyn, where they live at 1350 East 3rd Street, near Avenue M, in the same neighbourhood as his mother's two sisters, Annie Newman and Esther Balsam. Miller plants a pear tree in the backyard ('All I knew was cousins'). Celebrates his bar-mitzvah at the Avenue M Temple.

1930   Transfers from James Madison High School where he is reassigned to the newly built Abraham Lincoln High School on Ocean Parkway. Plays in the football team and injures his leg in a serious accident that will later excuse him from active military service. Academic record unimpressive, and he fails geometry twice.

1931   Early-morning delivery boy for a local bakery before going off to school; forced to stop when his bicycle is stolen. Works for his father during the summer vacation.

1933   Graduates from Abraham Lincoln High School and registers for night school at City College. He leaves after two weeks ('I just couldn't stay awake').

1933–   Earns $15 a week as a clerk for Chadwick-
34   Delamater, an automobile-parts warehouse in a run-

down section of Manhattan that will later become the site for the Lincoln Center for the Performing Arts. He is the only Jewish employee, and experiences virulent anti-Semitism for the first time.

1934   Writes to the Dean of the University of Michigan to appeal against his second rejection and says he has become a 'much more serious fellow' ('I still can't believe they let me in'). Travels by bus to Ann Arbor for the autumn semester, with plans to study journalism because 'Michigan was one of the few places that took writing seriously'. Lives in a rooming house on South Division Street and joins the *Michigan Daily* as reporter and night editor; takes a non-speaking part in a student production of Shakespeare's *King Henry VIII*. Moves to an attic room at 411 North State Street and works part-time in an off-campus laboratory feeding past-prime vegetables to thousands of mice.

1936   Writes his first play, *No Villain*, in six days during semester break and receives a Hopwood Award in Drama for $250 using the pseudonym 'Beyoum'. Changes his major to English.

1937   Enrols in Professor Kenneth T. Rowe's playwriting class. Rewrites *No Villain* as *They Too Arise* and receives a major award of $1,250 from the Theatre Guild's Bureau of New Plays (Thomas Lanier – later Tennessee – Williams was another winner in the same competition). *They Too Arise* is produced by the B'nai Brith Hillel Players in Detroit and at the Lydia Mendelssohn Theatre in Ann Arbor. Receives a second Hopwood Award for *Honors at Dawn* when Susan Glaspell is one of the judges. Contributes to *The Gargoyle*, the student humour magazine. Drives his college friend Ralph Neaphus east to join the Abraham Lincoln Brigade in the Spanish Civil War, but decides not to go with him. Months later Neaphus, twenty-three, was dead.

1938   Composes a prison play, *The Great Disobedience*, and revises *They Too Arise* as *The Grass Still Grows*. Graduates from the University of Michigan with a BA in English. Joins the Federal Theater Project in New York to write radio plays and scripts.

1939   The Federal Theater Project is shut down by conservative forces in Congress, and Miller goes on relief. Writes *Listen My Children* and *You're Next* with his friend and fellow

Michigan alumnus, Norman Rosten. *William Ireland's Confession* is broadcast on the Columbia Workshop.

1940   Marries Mary Grace Slattery, his college sweetheart at the University of Michigan. They move into a small apartment at 62 Montague Street in Brooklyn Heights. Writes *The Golden Years*, a play about Montezuma, Cortez, and the European conquest and corruption of Mexico. *The Pussycat and the Plumber Who Was a Man* airs on CBS Radio. Makes a trip to North Carolina to collect dialect speech for the Folk Division of the Library of Congress.

1941–   Works as a shipfitter's helper on the night shift at the
43   Brooklyn Navy Yard repairing battle-scarred war vessels from the North Atlantic fleet. Finishes additional radio plays, including *The Eagle's Nest* and *The Four Freedoms*. Completes *The Half-Bridge*. The one-act *That They May Win* is produced in New York.

1944   Daughter Jane is born. Prepares Ferenc Molnar's *The Guardsman* and Jane Austen's *Pride and Prejudice* for radio adaptation, and continues his own writing for the medium. Tours army camps in preparation for the draft of a screenplay called *The Story of G.I. Joe*, based on news reports written by the popular war correspondent Ernie Pyle (withdraws from the project when his role as author is compromised). Publishes *Situation Normal ...*, a book about this experience that highlights the real challenges returning soldiers encountered on re-entering civilian life. Dedicates the book to his brother, 'Lieutenant Kermit Miller, United States Infantry', a war hero. *The Man Who Had All the Luck* opens on Broadway but closes after six performances, including two previews. The play receives the Theater Guild National Award.

1945   Publishes *Focus*, a novel about anti-Semitism and moral blindness set in and around New York. His article 'Should Ezra Pound Be Shot?' appears in *New Masses*.

1946   Adapts *Three Men on a Horse* by George Abbott and John C. Holm for radio.

1947   *All My Sons* opens in New York and receives the New York Drama Critics' Circle Award; the Donaldson Award and the first Tony Award for best author. His son Robert is born. Moves with his family to a converted carriage house he purchases at 31 Grace Court in Brooklyn

Heights. Also buys a new car, a Studebaker, and a farmhouse in Roxbury, Connecticut. Writes the article 'Subsidized Theater' for the *New York Times*.

1948   Builds by himself a small studio on his Connecticut property where he writes *Death of a Salesman*. Edward G. Robinson and Burt Lancaster star in the film version of *All My Sons*.

1949   *Death of a Salesman*, starring Lee J. Cobb, Arthur Kennedy, Cameron Mitchell and Mildred Dunnock opens at the Morosco Theatre in New York on 10 February. Directed by Elia Kazan with designs by Jo Mielziner, it wins the New York Drama Critics' Circle Award, the Donaldson Prize, the Antoinette Perry Award, the Theatre Club Award and the Pulitzer Prize. His essay 'Tragedy and the Common Man' is printed in the *New York Times*. Attends the pro-Soviet Cultural and Scientific Conference for World Peace at the Waldorf-Astoria Hotel to chair a panel with Clifford Odets and Dimitri Shostakovich.

1950   Adaptation of Henrik Ibsen's *An Enemy of the People* produced on Broadway starring Fredric March and Florence Henderson ('I have made no secret of my early love for Ibsen's work'). First sound recording of *Death of a Salesman*. *The Hook*, a film script about graft and corruption in the closed world of longshoremen in the Red Hook section of Brooklyn, fails to reach production after backers yield to pressure from the House Committee on Un-American Activities. *On the Waterfront*, the Budd Schulberg–Elia Kazan collaboration featuring Marlon Brando, changes the setting to Hoboken, New Jersey, but is developed from the same concept, and is released four years later.

1951   Meets Marilyn Monroe. Fredric March in the role of Willy Loman for Columbia Pictures in the first film version of *Death of a Salesman*. Joseph Buloff translates the play into Yiddish; his production runs in New York and introduces Miller's play to Buenos Aires.

1952   Drives to Salem, Massachusetts, and visits the Historical Society, where he reads documents and researches the material he will use in *The Crucible*. Breaks with Kazan over the director's cooperation with HUAC.

1953   *The Crucible* wins the Donaldson Award and the Antoinette Perry Award when it opens in New York at the Martin Beck Theatre. Directs *All My Sons* in Arden, Delaware.

1954   US State Department denies Miller a passport to attend
the Belgian premiere of *The Crucible* in Brussels ('I wasn't
embarrassed for myself; I was embarrassed for my
country'). NBC broadcasts the first radio production of
Death of a Salesman. Mingei Theater stages first Japanese
translation of *Salesman* in Tokyo, where the play is
received as a cautionary tale about the 'salaryman'.

1955   The one-act version of *A View from the Bridge* opens in New
York on a double-bill with *A Memory of Two Mondays*.
HUAC pressurises city officials to withdraw permission
for Miller to make a film about juvenile delinquency set in
New York.

1956   Lives in Nevada for six weeks in order to divorce Mary
Slattery. Marries Marilyn Monroe. Subpoenaed to appear
before HUAC on 21 June, he refuses to name names.
Accepts an honorary degree as Doctor of Human Letters
from his alma mater, the University of Michigan. Jean-Paul
Sartre writes screenplay for French adaptation of *The
Crucible*, called *Les Sorcieres de Salem*; the film stars Yves
Montand and Simone Signoret. Travels with Monroe to
England, where he meets Laurence Olivier, her co-star in
The Prince and the Showgirl. Peter Brook directs revised two-
act version of *A View from the Bridge* in London at the New
Watergate Theatre Club, as censors determined it could
not be performed in public. 'Once Eddie had been
squarely placed in his social context, among his people,'
Miller noted, 'the myth-like feeling of the story emerged of
itself ... Red Hook is full of Greek tragedies.'

1957   Cited for contempt of Congress for refusing to co-operate
with HUAC. On the steps of the United States Congress,
and with Monroe on his arm, he vows to appeal against
the conviction. Monroe buys all members of Congress a
year's subscription to *I.F. Stone's Weekly*. First television
production of *Death of a Salesman* (ITA, UK). *Arthur Miller's
Collected Plays* is published, and his short story, 'The
Misfits', appears in *Esquire Magazine*.

1958–   The US Court of Appeals overturns his conviction
59   for contempt of Congress. Elected to the National
Institute of Arts and Letters and receives the Gold Medal
for Drama.

1961   Miller and Monroe divorce (granted in Mexico on the
grounds of 'incompatibility'). *The Misfits*, a black-and-

white film directed by John Huston featuring the actress in her first serious dramatic role, is released for wide distribution. Miller calls his scenario 'an eastern western' and bases the plot on his short story of the same name. Co-stars include Clark Gable, Montgomery Clift, Eli Wallach and Thelma Ritter. *The Crucible: An Opera in Four Acts* by Robert Ward and Bernard Stambler is recorded. Sidney Lumet directs a movie version of *A View from the Bridge* with Raf Vallone and Carol Lawrence. Miller's mother, Augusta, dies.

1962   Marries Austrian-born Inge Morath, a photographer with Magnum, the agency founded in 1947 by Henri Cartier-Bresson. Marilyn Monroe, aged thirty-six, dies. His daughter, Rebecca Augusta, is born in September. NBC broadcasts an adaptation of *Focus* with James Whitmore and Colleen Dewhurst.

1963   Publishes a children's book, *Jane's Blanket*. Returns to Ann Arbor to deliver annual Hopwood Awards lecture, 'On Recognition'.

1964   Visits the Mauthausen death camp with Inge Morath and covers the Nazi trials in Frankfurt, Germany, for the *New York Herald Tribune*. Reconciles with Kazan. *Incident at Vichy*, whose through-line is 'It's not your guilt I want, it's your responsibility', opens in New York, as does *After the Fall*. The former is the first of the playwright's works to be banned in the Soviet Union. The latter Miller says 'is not about Marilyn' and that she is 'hardly the play's *raison d'etre*'.

1965   Elected president of PEN, the international organisation of writers dedicated to fighting all forms of censorship. American premiere of the two-act version of *A View from the Bridge* is performed Off-Broadway. Laurence Olivier's production of *The Crucible*, starring Colin Blakely and Joyce Redman, is staged in London at the Old Vic by the National Theatre. Returns to Ann Arbor, where his daughter Jane is now a student, to participate in the first teach-in in the US concerning the Vietnam conflict.

1966   First sound recording of *A View from the Bridge*. In Rome Marcello Mastroianni and Monica Vitti play the parts of Quentin and Maggie in Franco Zeffirelli's Italian production of *After the Fall*. Miller's father, Isidore, dies.

1967   *I Don't Need You Any More*, a collection of short stories, is published. Sound recording of *Incident at Vichy*. Television production of *The Crucible* is broadcast on CBS. Visits Moscow and tries to persuade Soviet writers to join PEN. Playwright-in-Residence at the University of Michigan. His son, Daniel, is born in January.

1968   *The Price*, which the playwright called 'a quartet', 'the most specific play I've ever written', opens on Broadway. Sound recording of *After the Fall*. Attends the Democratic National Convention in Chicago as a delegate from Roxbury, Connecticut. Leads peace march against the war in South-East Asia with the Reverend Sloan Coffin, Jr, at Yale University in New Haven. *Death of a Salesman* sells its millionth copy.

1969   *In Russia*, a collaborative project with text by Miller and photography by Morath, is published. Visits Prague in a show of support for Czech writers; meets Vaclav Havel. Retires as president of PEN.

1970   Miller's works are banned in the Soviet Union, a result of his efforts to free dissident writers. *Fame* and *The Reason Why*, two one-act plays, are produced; the latter is filmed at his home in Connecticut.

1971   Television productions of *A Memory of Two Mondays* on PBS and *The Price* on NBC. Sound recording of *An Enemy of the People*. *The Portable Arthur Miller* is published.

1972   *The Creation of the World and Other Business* opens at the Schubert Theatre in New York on 30 November. Attends the Democratic National Convention in Miami as a delegate. First sound recording of *The Crucible*.

1973   PBS broadcasts Stacy Keach's television adaptation of *Incident at Vichy*, with Harris Yulin as Leduc. Champions the case of Peter Reilly, an eighteen-year-old falsely convicted of manslaughter for his mother's murder; four years later, all charges are dismissed. *After the Fall* with Faye Dunaway is televised on NBC. Teaches mini-course at the University of Michigan; students perform early drafts of scenes from *The American Clock*.

1974   *Up from Paradise*, musical version of *The Creation of the World and Other Business*, is staged at the Power Center for the Performing Arts at the University of Michigan. With music by Stanley Silverman and cover design by Al Hirschfield, Miller calls it his 'heavenly cabaret'.

1977   A second collaborative project with Inge Morath, *In the Country*, is published. Petitions the Czech government to halt arrests of dissident writers. The *Archbishop's Ceiling* opens at the Kennedy Center in Washington, DC. Miller said he wanted to dramatise 'what happens ... when people know they are ... at all times talking to Power, whether through a bug or a friend who really is an informer'.

1978   *The Theater Essays of Arthur Miller* is published. NBC broadcasts the film of *Fame* starring Richard Benjamin. Belgian National Theatre mounts the twenty-fifth anniversary production of *The Crucible*; this time Miller can attend.

1979   *Chinese Encounters*, with Inge Morath, is published. Michael Rudman directs a major revival of *Death of a Salesman* at the National Theatre in London, with Warren Mitchell as Willy Loman.

1980   *Playing for Time*, the film based on Fania Fenelon's autobiography *The Musicians of Auschwitz*, is broadcast nationally on CBS, with Vanessa Redgrave and Jane Alexander. ('I tried to treat it as a story meaningful to the survivors, by which I mean all of us. I didn't want it to be a mere horror story.') *The American Clock* has its first performance at the Spoleto Festival in South Carolina, then opens in New York with the playwright's sister, Joan Copeland, as Rose Baum, a role based on their mother. Miller sees his play as 'a mural', 'a mosaic', 'a story of America talking to itself ... There's never been a society that hasn't had a clock running on it, and you can't help wondering – How long?'

1981   Second volume of *Arthur Miller's Collected Plays* is published. Delivers keynote address on the fiftieth anniversary of the Hopwood Awards Program in Ann Arbor.

1982   Two one-act plays that represent 'the colors of memory', *Elegy for a Lady* and *Some Kind of Love Story*, are produced as a double-bill at the Long Wharf Theatre in Connecticut under the title *2 by A.M.*

1983   Directs *Death of a Salesman* at the People's Art Theatre in Beijing, part of a cultural exchange to mark the early stage of the opening of diplomatic relations between the United States and the People's Republic of China. Ying Ruocheng plays Willy Loman in his own Chinese translation. *I Think About You a Great Deal*, a monologue written as a tributre to Vaclav Havel, appears in *Cross Currents*, University of Michigan.

1984 *'Salesman' in Beijing* is published. The texts of *Elegy for a Lady* and *Some Kind of Love Story* are printed under a new title, *Two-Way Mirror*. Receives Kennedy Center Honors for lifetime achievement. Reworks the script of *The American Clock* for Peter Wood's London production at the National Theatre.

1985 Twenty-five million viewers see Dustin Hoffman play Willy Loman, with John Malkovich as Biff and Kate Reid as Linda in the production of *Death of a Salesman* shown on CBS. Goes to Turkey with Harold Pinter for PEN as an ambassador for freedom of speech. Serves as delegate at a meeting of Soviet and American writers in Vilnius, Lithuania, where he attacks Russian authorities for their continuing anti-Semitism and persecution of *samizdat* writers. *The Archbishop's Ceiling* is produced in the UK by the Bristol Old Vic. Completes adaptation of *Playing for Time* as a stage play.

1986 One of fifteen writers and scientists invited to meet Mikhail Gorbachev to discuss Soviet policies. The Royal Shakespeare Company uses a revised script of *The Archbishop's Ceiling* for its London production in the Barbican Pit.

1987 Miller publishes *Timebends: A Life*, his autobiography. Characterising it as 'a preemptive strike' against future chroniclers, he discusses his relationship with Marilyn Monroe in public for the first time. *Clara* and *I Can't Remember Anything* open as a double-bill at Lincoln Center in New York under the title *Danger: Memory!* Broadcasts of *The Golden Years* on BBC Radio and Jack O'Brien's television production of *All My Sons* on PBS. Michael Gambon stars as Eddie Carbone in Alan Ayckbourn's intimate production of *A View from the Bridge* at the National Theatre in London. University of East Anglia names its site for American Studies the Arthur Miller Centre.

1988 Publishes 'Waiting for the Teacher', a nineteen-stanza free-verse poem, in *Ha'aretz*, the Tel Aviv-based liberal newspaper, on the occasion of the fiftieth anniversary of the founding of the State of Israel.

1990 *Everybody Wins*, directed by Karel Reisz with Debra

Winger and Nick Nolte, is released: 'Through the evolution of the story – a murder that took place before the story opens – we will be put through an exercise in experiencing reality and unreality.' Television production of *An Enemy of the People* on PBS. Josette Simon plays Maggie as a sultry jazz singer in Michael Blakemore's London revival of *After the Fall* at the National Theatre, where *The Crucible* also joins the season's repertory in Howard Davies's production starring Zoë Wanamaker and Tom Wilkinson. Updated version of *The Man Who Had All the Luck* is staged by Paul Unwin in a joint production by the Bristol Old Vic and the Young Vic in London.

1991   *The Last Yankee* premieres as a one-act play. *The Ride Down Mount Morgan*, 'a moral farce', has its world premiere in London: 'The play is really a kind of nightmare.' Television adaptation of *Clara* on the Arts & Entertainment Network. Receives Mellon Bank Award for lifetime achievement in the humanities.

1992   *Homely Girl, A Life* is published with artwork by Louise Bourgeois in a Peter Blum edition. Writes satirical op-ed piece for the *New York Times* urging an end to capital punishment in the US. *The Last Yankee* receives its British premiere at the Young Vic.

1993   Expanded version of *The Last Yankee* opens at the Manhattan Theatre Club in New York. Television version of *The American Clock* on TNT with the playwright's daughter, Rebecca, in the role of Edie.

1994   *Broken Glass*, a work 'full of ambiguities' that takes 'us back to the time when the social contract was being torn up', has a pre-Broadway run at the Long Wharf Theatre in Connecticut; opens at the Booth Theatre in New York on 24 April. David Thacker's London production wins the Olivier Award for Best Play.

1995   Tributes to the playwright on the occasion of his eightieth birthday are held in England and the US. Receives William Inge Festival Award for Distinguished Achievement in American Theater. *Homely Girl, A Life and Other Stories*, is published. In England the collection appears under the title *Plain Girl*. Darryl V. Jones directs a production of *A View from the Bridge* in Washington, DC, and resets the play in a community of Domincan immigrants. The Arthur Miller Society is founded by Steve Centola.

1996   Revised and expanded edition of *The Theater Essays of
        Arthur Miller* is published. Receives the Edward Albee Last
        Frontier Playwright Award. Rebecca Miller and Daniel
        Day-Lewis are married.

1997   *The Crucible*, produced by the playwright's son, Robert A.
        Miller, is released for wide distribution and is nominated
        for an Academy Award. Revised version of *The Ride Down
        Mount Morgan* performed at the Williamstown Playhouse in
        Massachusetts. BBC airs television version of *Broken Glass*,
        with Margot Leicester and Henry Goodman repeating
        their roles from the award-winning London production.

1998   *Mr Peters' Connections* opens in New York with Peter Falk.
        Revival of *A View from the Bridge* by the Roundabout
        Theatre Company wins two Tony Awards. Revised
        version of *The Ride Down Mount Morgan* on Broadway.
        Miller is named Distinguished Inaugural Senior Fellow of
        the American Academy in Berlin.

1999   Robert Falls's fiftieth anniversary production of *Death of a
        Salesman*, featuring Brian Dennehy as Willy Loman, moves
        from the Goodman Theater in Chicago and opens on
        Broadway, where it wins the Tony Award for Best Revival
        of a Play. Co-authors the libretto with Arnold Weinstein
        for William Bolcom's opera of *A View from the Bridge*, which
        has its world premiere at the Lyric Opera of Chicago.

2000   Patrick Stewart reprises his role as Lyman Felt in *The Ride
        Down Mount Morgan* on Broadway, where *The Price* is also
        revived (with Harris Yulin). Major eighty-fifth birthday
        celebrations are organised by Christopher Bigsby at the
        University of East Anglia and by Enoch Brater at the
        University of Michigan, where plans are announced to
        build a new theatre named in his honour; it opens
        officially on 29 March 2007 ('whoever thought when I
        was saving $500 to come to the University of Michigan
        that it would come to this'). 'Up to a certain point the
        human being is completely unpredictable. That's what
        keeps me going … You live long enough, you don't rust.'
        Echoes Down the Corridor, a collection of essays from 1944 to
        2000, is published. Miller and Morath travel to Cuba
        with William and Rose Styron and meet Fidel Castro and
        the Colombian writer Gabriel García Márquez.

2001   Williamstown Theater Festival revives *The Man Who Had
        All the Luck*. Laura Dern and William H. Macy star in a

film based on the 1945 novel *Focus*. Miller is named the Jefferson Lecturer in the Humanities by NEH and receives the John H. Finley Award for Exemplary Service to New York City. His speech *On Politics and the Art of Acting* is published.

2002   Revivals in New York of *The Man Who Had All the Luck* and *The Crucible*, the latter with Liam Neeson as John Proctor. *Resurrection Blues* has its world premiere at the Guthrie Theatre in Minneapolis. Miller receives a major international award in Spain, the Premio Principe de Asturias de las Letras. Death of Inge Morath.

2003   Awarded the Jerusalem Prize. His brother, Kermit Miller, dies on 17 October. *The Price* is performed at the Tricycle Theatre in London.

2004   *Finishing the Picture* opens at the Goodman Theatre in Chicago. *After the Fall* revived in New York. Appears on a panel at the University of Michigan with Mark Lamos, who directs students in scenes from Miller's rarely performed plays.

2005   Miller dies of heart failure in his Connecticut home on 10 February. Public memorial service is held on 9 May at the Majestic Theatre in New York, with 1,500 in attendance. Asked what he wanted to be remembered for, the playwright said, 'A few good parts for actors.'

Commentary

When Willy Loman, suitcase in hand, walks slowly on to the set of *Death of a Salesman* in one of the most famous stage entrances in twentieth-century drama, he begins the long requiem that finally announces itself as such in the play's closing moments. The work, Arthur Miller said, 'is written from the sidewalk instead of from the skyscraper'. Unlike Willy's two sons, the audience hardly needs to wait for his wife's pronouncement to understand that 'the man is exhausted. A small man can be just as tired as a great man'. The playwright's proletarian spirit permeates the entire drama. Willy Loman, the salesman working on commissions that no longer come, is down on his luck, not that he really ever had any. Happy, who talks big, is the perpetual assistant to his company's assistant; Biff, who (unlike his father) knows that he's 'a dime a dozen', is the ageing, fair-haired boy gone to seed; and their mother, Linda, the homebody, ignored by time and the men around her, is unable to stem the tide that soon engulfs them all, try as she might. The whole question of 'Tragedy and the Common Man', the subject of one of the playwright's seminal essays of the same period, is neatly captured in the play's evocative subtitle, '*Certain Private Conversations in Two Acts and a Requiem*'.

Salesman's immediacy, accessibility and inter-generational appeal is a final tribute to Linda's great moment of lucidity, which occurs early in the play: 'Attention, attention must finally be paid to such a man.' Miller's challenge was formidable: how to construct a play that was on the one hand anecdotal and particular, and on the other widely and richly representative, symbolic, at times even mythic. From early on, the work originally called *The Inside of His Head* seemed to cry out for a practical stage solution as difficult and innovative as it was elusive: how to render the past, the present and the protagonist's increasingly desperate imaginings as one continuous whole, without resorting to mechanical 'flashbacks' (a term the playwright disliked). *Salesman*'s tone here is realistic, but it presupposes a realism with a marked difference. The naturalistic set Miller relied upon for his previous success, *All My Sons*, would no longer serve his purpose. To make this play work, stage space would have to be explored imaginatively, recalibrated and in fact reinvented. His much-celebrated collaboration with the director Elia Kazan and the brilliant designer Jo Mielziner resulted in the construction of a highly atmospheric platform set that gave *Salesman* the look and flexibility its narrative drive demanded. On a multi-level set time past and time present could be in constant dialogue with one another as a rhythmic pattern of renegotiation instantly emerged. All that was needed to signal temporal transition was stage lighting, accompanied by the sound of a flute playing somewhere in the distance. Given such a highly unusual design concept, Miller's '*dream rising out of reality*' could be rendered concrete, material and dead-centre – on stage.

No one involved in the original production of *Death of a Salesman* in 1949, least of all the author, was sure that the gamble would work. The producer Kermit Bloomgarden, one of the play's principal backers, recommended a different title for the play. Convinced that no one would buy a ticket to a show with 'death' advertised on the marquee, he suggested *Free and Clear* as an alternative, highlighting Linda's speech in the Requiem, which brings closure to the play. The playwright refused: 'The work I wrote is called *Death of a Salesman*.' When the curtain came down on the first night of the out-of-town tryout in Philadelphia, followed by an awkward silence, the tension, as Miller relates in his autobiography *Timebends*, was palpable and real. A lot was at stake, not only for Miller, but 'for the future of the American theatre'. There was, finally, thunderous applause, followed by the oddest thing of all: 'men and women wept openly' and, after the applause died down, 'members of the audience refused to leave and started talking to complete strangers about how deeply they had been affected by the play'. Miller, who thought he had written a tough, hard-hitting exposé of the dangerous and deceptive myth of 'making it in America', was entirely unprepared for the emotional punch *Salesman* delivered in performance. His play had at once found a life of its own.

The strong effect *Death of a Salesman* continues to have on Miller's audiences can be so daunting, the emotions it excites so raw, that the drama quickly becomes, despite its author's stated intentions, something quite different from a thesis play. And this may have little to do with the protagonist's socio-economic status as the quintessential 'low man'. The playwright took the name from Fritz Lang's *The Testament of Dr Mabuse*, the 1933 film in which a detective hopes to redeem himself by exposing a gang of forgers. Duped by them instead, he shouts into a telephone to his former boss, 'Lohmann! Help me for God's sake! Lohmann!' Later in the same film, we meet the crazed detective in the asylum as he shouts into an invisible phone, 'Lohmann? Lohmann? Lohmann?' 'What the name really meant to me,' Miller said, 'was a terrified man calling into the void for help that will never come.' And thinking about his own Loman in the notebook he kept while working on the first draft for the play, he wrote this: 'Remember [the character's] size', his 'ugliness'. 'Remember his attitude.' 'Remember', above all, '*pity*'.

Although we generally think of Miller as a playwright with a narrative rather than a visual imagination, *Death of a Salesman* relies on a profound sense of stage imagery: the set is Miller's play. Dwarfed by looming apartment blocks that rob the sunlight from Willy's garden (as well as his soul), the Loman house belongs to some other moment in time and a very different sense of place. What threatens both is impermanence and the flux of change. America is on the move, but the Loman sanctuary stands still. This is still Brooklyn, but a reimagined borough in which windows, like so many threatening eyes, stare down on a diminished world that seems ever more diminished and inconsequential. 'There's more people now!' Willy cries out in an anger that is really a sign of his despair. 'Bricks and windows, windows and bricks' frame his claustrophobia, which the set renders as agonisingly real. Music, too, tells the story. Each of Willy's journeys into the past, including one double journey, is signalled by the sound of a single, plaintive flute. His father, significantly, made his own flutes by hand, then sold them from a wagon by himself, always on the move. Willy's suitcase carries unspecified 'samples' of factory-made goods. Other sounds will be similarly evocative and similarly advance the plot. The recorded sound of a child on tape reciting the capital of every state in alphabetical order drowns out Willy's cry for help, and Biff is cautioned against whistling in elevators (he does so anyway; the Lomans are great whistlers and they all say 'Gee', a boy's word, not a man's). Finally, when Willy's life come crashing down all around him, we hear the '*frenzy of sound*' as his car starts up and races away, ominously, at full speed. What follows his 'accident' is '*the soft pulsation of a single cello string*'.

In *Salesman*, as elsewhere in the Miller repertory, the play's atmospheric dimension is there to enhance the work's narrative authority and appeal. This is first and foremost the theatre's most compelling representation of the dark underside of the so-called American Dream. Here it is rendered as half-fantasy, half-phantasmagoria, configured as it is as some triumphalist and everywhere disturbing guy-culture. Willy, as we are told in the Requiem, 'never knew who he was'. But he was also, as Miller said elsewhere, a man who 'chased everything that rusts'. He had 'all the wrong dreams'. Caught up, like most of post-war America, in the vain and unobtainable lure of success, which he equates with material wealth, popularity and the making of a good impression ('be well liked and you shall never want'), he realises all too late that what he has been searching for all his life he has had all along, and this is something that is not negotiable: Biff's unqualified love. What makes the play a tragedy – and it is certainly that – is that the father's unfulfilled ambitions, rather than any insurance premiums, are the only inheritance he can offer his sons. His legacy is their peril. 'I'm not bringing home any more prizes.' What Biff is saying is that you will have to love me anyway. But by that time it is too late. Willy drives off and kills himself. In *Death of a Salesman* Miller transforms Greek tragedy and brings it down, crashing, to earth.

Plot Summary, Structure And Dramatic Style

It is all but impossible in *Death of a Salesman* to separate the plot line from the highly stylised structure through which it has been carefully designed for maximum theatrical effect. Much is told through Willy's point of view, and the scenes sited in the past are nearly always, though not exclusively, his. In the frequently staged moments of his selective memory that seem to merge spontaneously and seamlessly into the present, we are literally, not figuratively, 'inside his head'. In such instances anything resembling an objective point of view is hard to pin down. The play builds its momentum symphonically, through the rich intersection of what Willy chooses to remember, how he remembers it, and other memories that he struggles to suppress but that intrude nonetheless. The other characters in the play, who also appear as figures in his past, bear witness in the present, as we do, to his increasing inability to locate the logical boundaries imposed by time, place and the contingencies of resolving a single dramatic action. The taut line of tension is sustained by observing them observe him. Willy's memories move swiftly to the rhythm of their own ebb and flow, but they follow very closely the expository demands of each dramatic encounter; their staging, however, requires a far more concrete system of synchronisation. Miller relies on a surprising new framework for narrative continuity, employing a deft transformation of apparent discontinuity: the plot develops through an atmospheric rather than a strictly linear arc. Plot summary, therefore, rarely does justice to the movement and meaning of this landmark play, though it is worth considering how economical the author has been in building so many resonances into the events that dramatically unfold.

Act One

Miller's stage directions for the opening of the play are a marvel of invention and display his dramatic imagination at full stretch. Everything is geared to tone, mood, atmosphere and gesture, and it is impossible to understand all that follows without an appreciation of the strategy outlined here. The emphasis is on lighting and lyricism, for this stage space has an '*air of dream*' that '*clings to the place, a dream rising out of reality*'. The play begins in silence, as all plays do, but that silence is soon interrupted when a melody is heard, '*played upon a flute*'. Significantly, '*It is small and fine, telling of grass and trees and the horizon*' as the curtain slowly rises on a set that seems to come from another world entirely: the salesman's house, surrounded by '*towering*', '*angular*', even '*angry*' shapes on all sides. In the ominous shadows cast by encroaching apartment blocks – the stage direction calls them, tellingly, '*vaults*' – the Loman house makes its last stand, out-of-date and out of time, as a '*small, fragile-seeming home*'. Oddly enough, the lines that follow detail the nuts-and-bolts multidimensionality of the platform set, as Miller turns his attention to the logistics of the *mise-en-scène*. Place and placement are designed for flexibility and impermeability. Abandoning the narrow constraints of fourth-wall realism, Miller prepares the stage for scenes that blend swiftly and unobtrusively one into the other, then another. Such spaces must be everywhere configured to accommodate themselves not only to the specific locations for the actions that follow (kitchen, boys' bedrooms, parents' bedroom, garden, backyard, office, restaurant, hotel room), but equally so – and perhaps even more crucially so – to time past, time present and time remembered. It is into this deliberately staged world that Willy Loman enters, tired and exhausted. And as he does so, carrying two large sample suitcases, he is first and foremost an image before he is a personality.

Willy crosses the stage to the doorway of the house, unlocks the door and, muttering to himself, enters the kitchen. He occupies these spaces with authority; each of his movements defines them for the audience before he moves

into the offstage living-room, where he will deposit his bags.
As he does so, the focus turns to Linda, who has stirred in
her bed in another stage space on the right. She has heard
her husband come in unexpectedly, and *'with some trepidation'*
cries out the play's first real line of dialogue, 'Willy!' Their
encounter relays pivotal information: she's worried that he
may have 'smash[ed]' the car; he tells her that he was on his
way but just 'couldn't make it', couldn't drive any more; and
she tries to mollify him by suggesting any number of excuses
for his sudden return ('the steering again', 'you never went
for your new glasses', and most revealing of all in terms of
dramatic foreshadowing, 'Well, you'll just have to take a
rest, Willy, you can't continue this way'). Willy hardly hears
her as he recites his first of many monologues, this one
detailing what happened to him on the road when he
'opened the windshield' and 'let the warm air bathe over
me'. 'I have such thoughts, I have such strange thoughts.'
Willy is confused; later in the same scene he will rebuke
Linda for even mentioning the removable windshield, for
that clumsy apparatus belonged to the model he owned
years before, not the one he drives off the road now. It is
through a reliance on seemingly minor details like this that
Miller begins to establish key elements of his plot (later in
the play silk stockings play a similar role, those darned by
Linda and the new ones given to his mistress in a Boston
hotel room). Their discussion turns to the practical, at least
on Linda's part, as the couple begins to speculate on his
chances for shifting his sales 'territory' from New England to
more local markets in New York. Willy isn't really
interested: 'They don't need me in New York. I'm the New
England man. I'm vital in New England.' What Willy fears
is change.

But this isn't any ordinary evening, and not just because
Willy has been unable to make a sales trip. Biff, the one-
time golden boy whose sports trophies are getting dusty, has
come home. His lack of completion is just as troubling:
thirty-four years old, he is still not able to '[find] himself'.
Father and son have already had one of their brutal
encounters before the play began: an argument which took

place just after Biff got off the train from nowhere in
particular. Their antagonism – and the history behind it –
forms the basis of the play's rising action, though at this
early point in the drama it serves as a device to establish
conflict and expose psychological texture.

Both of these elements are considerably amplified as stage
lighting illuminates yet another space, this one the raised
platform outlining the dimensions of Biff and Happy's
childhood bedroom. This is an unusual place in which to
find two physically grown men, and yet it is the perfect
setting in which to localise their emotional paralysis and
perennial adolescence. Each son is stunted in his own way:
Happy, who usually sleeps in his own bachelor apartment, is
more 'bum' than playboy, and Biff, more 'guy' than 'man',
still uses words like 'gee' and 'naa' and 'pal'. The vocabulary
they use as they listen across their twin beds to their parents'
give-and-take – Willy gives and Linda takes – is laced with
wished-for macho wonders that turn out to be more like
blunders. Even they can barely disguise the changes that
have come over them: 'I don't know' – and Biff is probably
speaking for both of them at this point – 'what I'm supposed
to want.' Happy shies away from self-reflection like this, and
tries hard to avoid it throughout the play; though his
brother, the former high-school football hero – he peaked
much too soon – can be cauterised by his awareness of the
waste he is making of his own life. Yet once together, they
spur one another on to create another childlike fantasy, this
one quintessentially American: moving together 'out West',
raising cattle, using their 'muscles', and ripping off their
shirts in the middle of a hot afternoon in Montana or
Nevada or Arizona or some other place that ends in an 'a'
where people couldn't locate Brooklyn on a map, even if
they wanted to.

Their reverie is cut short when they hear from below that
their father is talking to himself, memorialising and
sentimentalising a past he tries so desperately to recapture.
This is nostalgia writ large. The scene not only shifts back to
the kitchen, then to the garden, but more significantly to the
past; this is the first of the play's many temporal leaps. Biff

and Happy must now play down, performing the younger versions of themselves their father so much longs for them to be again. Their shared past is a world of football passes, hammocks, punching bags, sneakers, college logos, Simonised cars, youthful vigour, firm male bodies, inevitable sunshine – the way it was or should have, could have been. It never rains in the past (though the skies will turn dark for Willy's funeral).

And yet there is a serpent in every garden, including Willy Loman's. The site of his elaborate myth-making is quickly and fatally compromised even in this first journey into the rosy past, and it is accomplished by the smallest of gestures – a 'borrowed' football from the high-school locker room ('The coach told me to practice my passing'); Biff's plan to up-end his team's passing game by taking off his helmet and 'breakin' out' for an unauthorised touchdown; Biff's driving without a licence; above all the threat of failing maths. To his son's questionable behaviour Willy offers no repudiation; in fact, he encourages it, filling Biff with an unearned sense of self-esteem and its corollary, success-at-any-price, even if it means bending the rules or worse: lie, cheat, steal and deceive. 'Be liked and you shall never want' is Willy's false mantra, and he has stuffed his sons, as they say in Brooklyn, 'full of it'. Make 'an appearance', create 'personal interest' and the world will be their oyster because they are – what? – 'both built like Adonises'. Biff, the captain of the team, will always be in first place, or so his father makes him believe.

What the Lomans are full of is talk: Willy exaggerates the number of his commissions, misrepresents the amount he earns, puffs up his position in the firm and fantasises about his popularity with the buyers. Yet he knows he is 'fat' and 'foolish to look at', and behind his back he heard another salesman liken him to a 'walrus'. However, Linda still thinks him 'the handsomest man in the world'. No matter, in either case. Biff will be his redemption. Suddenly, strange laughter is heard '*to the left of the house*': 'The Woman' comes into full view from behind a scrim, exposing herself and the charade of domestic tranquility. In his imagination and in the stage blocking Willy moves into this new scene before Linda's laughter merges with the Woman's and returns him to the kitchen. We're still in the past, but we have just made a double journey into it.

As Linda exits, the scene returns to the present. Happy comes down the stairs in his pyjamas and discovers his father still talking to himself. Willy, returning to everyday reality, gradually becomes aware of his son's presence and rehearses with him the 'awful scare' he had today that brought him back home: 'Nearly hit a kid in Yonkers.' What he yearns for is release, some alternative existence, the one he might have had with the myth-like figure of his brother Ben.

The scene becomes more complicated with the arrival of Willy's neighbour, Charley, who is also the only friend he has ever had. The kind-hearted Charley invites himself into the house because he is worried about Willy, having just heard disturbing noises in the night. They play a game of cards to while away the time, but the tricks go awry when Willy 'sees' Ben walk, umbrella in hand, straight into the set. Willy must now carry on a double conversation, one with his uneasy casino partner, the other with an apparition from his past. Charley, growing impatient with the lack of connection, gives up on him, picks up the cards and departs. Willy is now free to move directly into his dream-world, and as he does so he brings his whole family, as well as a younger version of Charley, with him. In this key scene, re-drawing the lines of the past on the space before us, a number of important details quickly accumulates: Linda meets Willy's brother for the first time and is unsure about him, as well as critical of his underhand sportsmanship in boxing with a teenage Biff, whom he humiliates. Ben, another great talker ('William, when I walked into the jungle, I was seventeen. When I walked out I was twenty-one. And, by God, I was rich!'), also relates the flamboyant history of the boys' grandfather, 'a wild-hearted' flute-maker and inventor of gadgets, and a travelling man who rarely stayed in one place for very long. Willy longs to spend more time with his elder brother and find out something more, anything more, about a father he has never really known: 'Dad left when I was such a baby and I never had a chance to talk to him and I still feel – kind of temporary about myself.' Details like this add a great deal of poignancy to the dramatic moment, just as they serve to open up and expand the psychological range of the drama as a whole.

Linda re-enters, signalling our return to the present. Willy, still reeling from the mental encounter with his brother, asks about the diamond watch fob he gave him when he visited the family from Africa, and she reminds him that they pawned it long ago. Willy's departure for a late-night walk, shuffling away in his slippers, clears the stage for the famous confrontation scene she has been waiting to have with her two negligent and (in different ways) troubled sons.

The scene brings us to the very heart of Miller's drama. What it reveals so clearly is that Linda's allegiance is to her husband before it is to her sons. As the opening stage directions have already told us, '*she more than loves him, she admires him, as though his mercurial nature, his temper, his massive dreams and little cruelties, served her only as sharp reminders of the turbulent longings within him, longings which she shares but lacks the temperament to utter and follow to their end.*' As her sons descend the stairs to enter her space, the well-kept kitchen, Biff attempts to establish her as a potential ally and partial confidante (he will, of course, not tell her everything – what happened in Boston remains strictly off-limits), while Happy plays the choral part, backing up his brother. Linda steadfastly resists their manoeuvres, and displays her metal even further by repudiating them, most especially Biff, the son Willy adores, for their 'hateful' treatment of their father, a man crying out for help: 'Biff, dear' – and her line is loaded – 'if you don't have any feeling for him, then you can't have any feeling for me.' One of Miller's great strengths as a writer of stage dialogue is on display here: his ability to find eloquence even in the rhythms of everyday speech. Linda's lines that follow, for example, say more about the entire issue of 'tragedy and the common man' than anything the playwright or his critics have had to say about it elsewhere:

> I don't say he's a great man. Willy Loman never made a lot of money. His name was never in the paper. He's not the finest character that ever lived. But he's a human being, and a terrible thing is happening to him. So attention must be paid. He's not to be allowed to fall into his grave like an old dog. Attention, attention must be finally paid to such a person. You called him crazy . . . a lot of people think he's lost his balance. But you don't have to be very smart to know what his trouble is. The man is exhausted . . . A small man can be just as exhausted as a great man. (pp. 44–5)

So convincing is Linda's moving speech that she even succeeds in turning Biff around, at least temporarily: he'll find a job and stay at home now, a declaration that seems even more heartfelt once he learns that his father has been trying to kill himself. There is, nonetheless, an important caveat: Biff insists that his mother should not blame everything on him. 'What happened to the love you had for him? You were such pals!' a distraught Linda cries out in an emotional outburst that reveals as much about her momentary insecurity as it does about her anger. The answer to that question will be the furtive through-line that keeps the rest of the play going.

Linda's big scene also reveals something else that is fundamental to the dynamics of this family drama: her unacknowledged complicity in its steady unravelling. As powerful as her speech is – it more than adequately conveys her anxiety about Willy, her real fear of the emptiness that awaits her if he is no longer there, as well as the play's central thesis – it nevertheless encapsulates the extent to which she has been the enabler of Willy's self-delusions. She has not only put up with the disgraceful way he treats her (no wonder Happy talks about women with such disrespect), but she has made excuses for her husband all her life long. Worse still, she has never intervened when Willy filled their sons with so many illusions of grandeur, not to mention the imbalance with which he has meted out his affection for them. Happy has been, at best, an afterthought. Much of this remains deeply buried in the play's subtext, even in this critical scene. These disturbing tensions are in any case quickly overwhelmed by others when Willy, who has overheard Biff in the last part of the scene, delivers his Parthian shot: 'Even your grandfather was better than a carpenter. You never grew up.'

As the act draws to a close, it is important for Miller to demonstrate the *modus operandi* of this family's customary but still lethal dysfunctionality: Biff takes the bait and once again assumes his assigned role as his father's main antagonist; Linda engages in her vain attempt to calm the waters, and is promptly put down for it; Happy interjects with the bright promise of a new day dawning, a business opportunity for the Loman brothers – 'sporting goods'; and Willy turns around and betters Happy's feisty game plan. Then, as always, and almost without noticing that they are doing so, the characters turn on one another. Willy stalks off, followed by the transference of guilt and the inevitable, vain apologies. The pattern is bound to reinscribe itself: 'you got a greatness in you,' Willy serenades Biff, 'remember that. You got all kinds a greatness . . .' He's still 'like a young god', a 'Hercules – something like that', he confides to Linda. 'And the sun, the sun all around him . . . God Almighty, he'll be great yet. A star like that, magnificent, can never really fade away!' Earlier in the act it was Happy who said that his brother was 'a poet'. But it is really their father, *'staring through the window into the moonlight'*, who lyricises his feelings as the curtain slowly falls: 'Gee, look at the moon moving between the buildings!' This luminous nightscape, however, comes with a cautionary note: Biff takes the tubing with which his father has tried to kill himself and walks quickly up the stairs.

Act Two
The scene opens with the dual promise that both father and son, now reconciled (for the moment, at least) will move forward with their plans for the future: Biff will meet Bill Oliver and Willy will meet Howard, the young man who

has inherited the family business. As the curtain rises, the music is '*gay and bright*', a sharp contrast to the lone sound of a flute that frames our entry into the opening of the play. The action is set in the kitchen, the site of so much of the turmoil and confrontation that has taken place in the first act, but here the mood is positive, generative, even comforting. Willy sits at the table sipping coffee, he dreams of planting his garden again, and the whole house smells of shaving lotion: the Loman boys are already out and away. Yet such textures can be deceptive. Linda notes that Biff looked 'so handsome' in his blue suit when he left the house early that morning, before her husband was even awake. Later in the act we will learn that Biff was recently in jail for three months for stealing a suit very much like the one he is wearing today.

Miller builds this act on the foundations he has carefully laid in everything that occurs in the preceding scenes. And it's the attention to the small details in the ominous undertones of the previous dramatic action that will soon overtake this one as well. Money's short: the Studebaker's recent 'motor job' still hasn't been paid for, the refrigerator needs a new fan belt and, most significantly of all, the premium on Willy's life insurance is overdue (Linda reminds him that they're in 'the grace period now').

Everything they own has been purchased on 'time'; and by the time everything's paid off, everything's broken. Linda reminds Willy of one more item, the one that will come to haunt her at the play's conclusion: the final installment on their mortgage. 'After this payment, Willy, the house belongs to us.'

Willy departs, but not before several homely reminders: Linda cautions him to be careful on the subway stairs, to take his saccharine and his glasses, to be sure to meet Biff and Happy for dinner at Frank's Chop House. The telephone rings as Linda is left alone on stage; her one-sided conversation with Biff is filled with both disappointment and the frailest of hope. She discovers that it was Biff, not Willy, who removed the fateful attachment to the gas heater, but his high spirits as he just left the house have nonetheless buoyed her. 'Be sweet to him tonight, dear,' she implores her son, '*trembling with sorrow and joy*', 'Be loving to him. Because he's only a little boat looking for a harbor.' In the middle of her speech the light fades on her as the scene shifts to Howard's office. Willy has appeared, but Howard barely notices him, intent as he is on threading a new tape into his latest acquisition, a voice-recording machine. We already know this is all going to end badly for Willy Loman.

And it does. Each of his appeals for what Linda has just called a safe 'harbor' is summarily dismissed. Howard is cruel, with the cruelty and insensitivity of a young man who has always had it good and has never had to grub for a living – or for anything else for that matter. Yet he reminds us, too, that Willy has never been that much of an earner; he never made the sales or commissions he brags about and, after all, 'business is business'; 'everybody's gotta pull his own weight'. Willy romanticises a time when there was 'friendship' and 'personality' in this very same office; but it is in this same space, instead, that he is now fired. The scene's framing device is the sound of a child's voice reciting the names of the capital of every state in alphabetical order, and the irony cuts to the quick, adding insult to injury. But not before Miller provides Willy with a stunning monologue, the one that gives him the title for his play:

> . . . my father lived many years in Alaska. He was an adventurous man. We've got quite a little streak of self-reliance in our family. I thought I'd go out with my older brother and try to locate him, and maybe settle in the North with the old man. And I was almost decided to go, when I met a salesman in the Parker House. His name was Dave Singleman. And he was eighty-four years old, and he'd drummed merchandise in thirty-one states. And old Dave, he'd go up to his room, y'understand, put on his green velvet slippers – I'll never forget – and pick up his phone and call the buyers, and without ever leaving his room, at the age of eighty-four, he made his living. And when I saw that, I realised that selling was the greatest career a man could want. 'Cause what could be more satisfying than to be able to go, at the age of eighty-four, into twenty or thirty different cities, and pick up the phone, and be remembered and loved and helped by so many different

people? Do you know? when he died – and by the way he died
the death of a salesman, in his green velvet slippers in the
smoker of the New York, New Haven and Hartford, going
into Boston – when he died, hundreds of salesman and buyers
were at his funeral. Things were sad on a lotta trains for
months after that . . . In those days there was personality in it,
Howard. There was respect, and comradeship, and gratitude
in it. Today, it's all cut and dried, and there's no chance for
bringing friendship to bear – or personality. You see what I
mean? They don't know me any more. (p. 66)

This resonant monologue serves as a stirring counterweight
to Linda's in the previous act; but as Willy brings an all but
mythic dimension to the art of selling, embodied as he still
sees it in a heroic figure from the past, Howard hardly looks
up at him: 'Now pay attention!' he suddenly cries out, and
his anger is justified. His language can be just as pointed,
and as eloquent in an entirely different way, when Miller
provides him with lines heavily inflected by the rhythms of
New York speech: 'I put thirty-four years into this firm,
Howard, and now I can't pay my insurance! You can't eat
the orange and throw the peel away – a man is not a piece
of fruit!' Using a metaphor without ever realising that he is
doing so, he, too, like Linda, demands that 'attention' – and
the word has been carefully chosen – must be paid. His
voice falls on deaf ears. 'Whenever you can this week,'
Howard intones, disenfranchising him completely, 'stop by
and drop off the samples.'

   As Willy stares blankly into space, Ben's music, '*first
distinctly, then closer, closer*', all at once intrudes, signalling yet
another retreat into the past. The scene rehearses the fateful
visit when Ben made his final appeal for Willy to join him.
'He's got a beautiful job here,' Linda interjects, revealing
her own complicity in holding him back. 'Don't say those
things to him!' she states firmly, even adamantly. 'Enough to
be happy right here, right now.' The moment is
inopportune all around; Biff, the golden boy, is about to
have his tryouts at Ebbets Field. Happy as well as Charley's
son Bernard are beside themselves with excitement, though
Charley himself introduces a note of caution, if not

downright ridicule. Willy counters this by characterising his neighbour's remarks as entirely out of bounds, and declares that for his son 'This is the greatest day of his life.' It is; but no one on stage yet realises just how potent the line is in dramatic irony.

The scene that follows is a sombre one. We are now in the present, in the reception room of Charley's office. A great deal of the play's back story is revealed: Charley has been handing out money to Willy so that he can pretend to Linda that he is still an adequate, albeit marginal, provider. Bernard, the worrier and the studier, now grown up and working as an accomplished attorney on his way to Washington, DC, to argue a case before the United States Supreme Court, is present, too. And it is this figure from Biff's boyhood past who asks the crucial questions: why was Biff so changed when he came back from Boston? What happened there? Why didn't Biff take the summer make-up course when he 'flunked' high-school maths? The audience already knows that before the curtain comes down on this drama the answers to all of Bernard's questions will be made painfully clear, though Miller keeps the suspense going by not giving away more than he has to at this point. There's another kind of drama going on in this scene anyway; Willy refuses the job Charley offers him because he sees this as his final humiliation.

Little does he see that there's more to come. 'Raucous music' and 'a red glow' bring us to the restaurant where Willy is to meet his sons for a celebratory dinner. Happy is discovered on stage with a waiter, and the setup provides him with the opportunity to display his credentials as small-time operator and pathetic 'philanderer', the word his mother has already used to characterise his refusal to accept any responsibility for his actions. Before Willy and Biff arrive on the scene, he tells the waiter that his brother is an important 'cattle man' from the Far West, and plays the role of big-time spender when he propositions a young woman and tells her a different tale about his brother's status, now configured as a professional football player. Biff appears, and 'the Girl' soon exits to 'make a phone call' to complete what she assumes will be a wild night out. She is not on stage to hear about his diminished state: he waited six hours to see Bill Oliver, then finally saw him for 'one minute' as he left his office. 'I realised what a ridiculous lie my whole life has been!' he confesses. 'We've been talking in a dream for fifteen years.' All he can do now is repeat the self-destructive pattern that has never been broken: this time he finds his way into Oliver's office, steals a pen and runs down 'all eleven flights' of stairs. Yet he knows instinctively that something must now change: 'Hap, I'm gonna tell Pop.'

What Biff has in mind is nothing less than full exposure of the kind of 'life lie' that has haunted the Loman family forever. Happy says he's 'crazy'; they must protect their father at all costs. When Willy comes into the restaurant a few moments later, Biff seems more determined than ever. But his determination is slowly undermined as Willy reveals that he has been fired and the cycle of deception and denial asserts itself once again. Happy is only too willing to aid and abet, editing his brother's commentary and finally distorting it completely, Willy only too willing to fall back into their mutual fantasy. Biff is undone. But not more so than his father as a *single trumpet jars the ear*. Young Bernard enters crying 'Mrs Loman, Mrs Loman!', forcing Willy to remember the painful day when they got the news that Biff 'had to go and flunk math'. But only Willy relives the scene. Biff and Happy are still in the present. 'What math?' Biff demurs. 'What're you talking about?' Willy is both in and out of the present, more out than in, as the past replays itself kaleidoscopically. Young Bernard announces to Linda that Biff has run off to Boston to see his father. 'Oh, maybe Willy can talk to the teacher,' Linda suggests, participating as she has always done in the family game of illusion and reality. In the meantime, Willy hasn't really heard a word of what Biff has been trying to say, as the scene from the past he has so much wanted to repress begins to insinuate its ugly presence. 'Standish Arms, good evening!' the voice of a hotel telephone operator declares from the vast nowhere. 'I'm not in my room!' Willy shouts on stage. Biff is suddenly frightened: 'Dad, what's the matter?' And as the stage

directions tell us, Biff is not only frightened, but horrified.
He falls down on one knee before his father and utters the
very words he had promised himself never to say again:
'Dad, I'll make good. I'll make good.' The lethal trap in
which they find themselves has no exit.

At least not yet. The new presence on stage of Letta and
Miss Forsythe, who may or may not 'sell' (the former has
answered the latter's telephone summons to join the young
men), forces Willy to reactivate the sad moment when Biff
discovered him alone in a hotel room with 'The Woman'.
Biff took the train from Grand Central Station in New York
all the way up to Boston in order to seek his father's help –
surely Mr Birnbaum, the recalcitrant maths teacher with a
lisp, will succumb to Willy's charm when he speaks so
smoothly and persuasively on his son's behalf. Willy is his
son's hero after all; he will now become his saviour, too – or
so Biff imagines. The impressionable boy is forced to witness
a scene of adultery instead. Vain attempts at concealment
make matters even worse, as does the handing-over of a pair
of shiny silk stockings: 'You,' Biff cries out accusingly, 'you
gave her Mama's stockings!' 'You fake!', 'you – liar!', 'You
phony little fake!' soon follow. In this powerful scene,
father/son behaviour with women is, from a dramatic point
of view, very efficiently turned on its head. Biff, crestfallen,
returns to New York; and we can now piece together all of
the information we have been given leading up to this
fateful encounter. There's worse to come for Willy. Though
earlier Biff has told Miss Forsythe that she's 'just seen a
prince walk by. A fine troubled prince. A hardworking,
unappreciated prince. A pal, you understand? A good
companion' (p. 97), both sons have now carelessly
abandoned their father and taken off with their own
'chippies' instead. Stanley, the sympathetic waiter who lies
on their behalf, stuffs Willy's money back into his pocket
even though his sons have walked out without paying the
bill. Willy needs the cash; he wants to buy seeds to plant in
his garden one last time.

The sound of the flute is heard as light gradually rises on
the kitchen. The sons appear at the door; Linda is unseen,

but she has been waiting up for them all night. As she enters from the living-room, her fury is evident even before she speaks. Disgusted by their behaviour and their gift of appeasement, flowers, she knocks them to the floor at Biff's feet. To Happy she is even more unmerciful: 'Did you have to go to women tonight? You and your lousy rotten whores!' Miller handles this final scene of confrontation skilfully. Biff wants 'an abrupt conversation' with 'the boss', but Linda is determined to protect her husband from what she knows in advance will be his final undoing. All the while Willy, flashlight in hand, is planting seeds and talking about a 'proposition' to a Ben no longer remembered, but a Ben now fully imagined. 'Twenty thousand,' his brother considers, 'that *is* something one can feel with the hand, it is there.' That the 'twenty thousand' involves his insurance policy prepares us for how this play is going to end:

> Oh, Ben, how do we get back to all the great times? Used to be so full of light, and comradeship, the sleigh-riding in winter, and the ruddiness on his cheeks. And always some kind of good news coming up ahead. And never even let me carry the valises in the house, and simonizing, simonizing that little red car! Why, why can't I give him something and not have him hate me? (p. 109)

A monologue for Willy, but a soliloquy for us, what this moving speech reveals is that it is Biff, Biff, it has always been Biff.

What happens next is inevitable, only because Miller has made it so. Biff moves to the central position, finds his voice, and tells his father, simply, and in a great moment of self-revelation, 'I'm a dime a dozen.' But in what the text calls '*an uncontrolled outburst*', his father tries for one last time to counter such defeatism, shouting out – in despair? in agony? in frustration? all three? – 'I am not a dime a dozen. I am Willy Loman and you are Biff Loman!' Truth will out, nevertheless, even at this late date: Biff says his father was nothing 'but a hard-working drummer who landed in the ash can like all the rest of them.' As for Biff, 'I'm not bringing home any prizes any more, and you're going to

stop waiting for me to bring them home!' Their world of
illusions comes crashing down: 'Pop, I'm nothing! I'm
nothing, Pop . . . I'm just what I am, that's all . . . Will you
let me go?', and that final appeal is indeed 'remarkable'.
What Willy has been looking for he has always had all
along: his son's unqualified love.

The imaginary Ben summons Willy to his final action in
the play as his car speeds off.

Requiem
It should come as no real surprise that Miller, who has built
his play so deliberately to the accompaniment of a variety of
musical motifs, should choose to close *Salesman* with a scene
richly dependent on the kind of atmosphere we associate
with such master composers as Mozart, Verdi, and Fauré.
For a requiem, as in the one Beethoven wrote 'for a Fallen
Hero', is both a prayer and a homage to the dead. Here it
comes in the shape of a spare funeral scene, and one that
emerges virtually spontaneously from the sounds that signal
Willy's demise. Unlike the massive attendance for the
legendary Dave Singleman's memorial ceremony, Willy's
has had few attendants, only those whose emotional
attachment to him has always been fixed: his wife, his two
sons, and a single friend. 'He had the wrong dreams,' Biff
intones at his father's grave. 'He never knew who he was.'
Happy disagrees, but it is the faithful Charley who is the one
to speak in his friend's defence: 'Nobody dast blame this
man. A salesman is got to dream . . . It comes with the
territory.' Linda, carrying flowers like the ones she refused
to accept from her sons in the previous scene, somehow
cannot cry. But release will come, for Miller gives her the
curtain speech. Alone on stage, and finally occupying it with
authority, it is her words that echo in our ears as the curtain
slowly falls: 'Willy, I made the last payment on the house
today. Today, dear. And there'll be nobody home . . . We're
free and clear . . . We're free . . . We're free.'

Yet in the final movement of this haunting requiem, even
Linda's words are no longer necessary, for '*Only the music of*

the flute is left on the darkening stage as over the house the hard towers of the apartment buildings rise into sharp focus.'

Themes

One of the signature virtues of *Death of a Salesman*, and of Miller's work in general, is its ability to speak to audiences around the world with astonishing immediacy and clarity. The accessibility of the playwright's themes, and the multiple resonances his drama gives rise to, is especially notable in *Salesman*, the play which is, among many other things, about a man who lives in a dream and mistakes it for reality. The author's characterisation of his central figure has a way of monopolising many discussions about the play, and yet its position as one of the most significant works written for the American theatre should lead us to a number of other considerations as well, all of them interrelated. Some of these issues might be understood as follows:

'Tragedy and the Common Man'
The subject of a major essay by the playwright, which he wrote in response to the critical reception of *Salesman* when it first reached Broadway in 1949, tragedy as it might be experienced by the workaday, working man displays Miller's huge proletarian ambition for one of the major themes in his play. Willy Loman is designed to be a protagonist capable of sustaining the scope, depth and sheer dramatic tension traditionally associated with legendary figures from the grand theatrical past, a repertory that ranges widely and even includes figures of the heroic dimension of Oedipus and Lear. In *Death of a Salesman* Miller's indebtedness to the shape of tragedy in the theatrical past is everywhere apparent, as is his effectiveness in adapting its conventions to the scaled-down economies of the modern world. In the story that unfolds Miller emblematises the inescapability of tragedy by concentrating on elements that are little and

local, then discovers in them a symbolic dimension far
beyond the anecdotal. Willy's story is in the first instance
personal, as tragedy always is; yet its resonances stretch far
beyond a given time and a given place. The scene is
Brooklyn, 'Willy Loman territory', but it is a Brooklyn of the
imagination, dramatically transformed.

The American Dream: materialism, consumerism and happiness
It is probably something of a truism to say that *Death of a
Salesman* represents the dark underside of the so-called
American Dream, a phrase that originated in the early
1930s. As the play demonstrates time and time again, that
dream is likely to become a nightmare for individuals caught
in-between the dualities of an encroaching materialism and
the rampant consumerism it implies. Happiness is equated
with material success; anything less than being 'rich'
signifies failure. Willy fully buys into this myth, as well as its
deceptive corollaries: be liked and you shall never want,
look good and make an impression, be athletic, nice and
'manly'. This is the legacy he wills on his sons, handicapping
any chance they might have had to find out who they really
are or what they might have become under the influence of
a different father. Willy never realises until it is far too late
that 'business is business', a far more lethal game than
anything he has ever had in mind as the ticket to the
misbegotten 'success' that continues to elude him. Neither
does he have any sense that the growing corporate culture –
an unsentimental conglomerate of take-and-take, not give-
and-take – has stacked all the cards against him.

(Dysfunctional) family values
Because the Lomans have built their life together on denial
and deception – and, above all, on self-deception – it is only
a matter of time before fate, which they experience as
exposure – undoes them all. And because they have never
broken the cycle of denial and its deceptions, they are fated,
too, to rehearse their dysfunctional family dynamics over

and over again. Biff tries to break through the false values
that have corrupted him; he tries, then tries again. When he
finally succeeds in doing so – *if* he does so at the play's
conclusion – the price he pays is a heavy one indeed.

The great generational conflict of father and son

As in the play that precedes it, *All My Sons*, the mighty
antagonism in *Salesman* is embodied in another father and
son, Willy and Biff Loman. Their battle, too, is a fight to the
finish, for each represents a different version of what it
means to be truly alive in this world. That battle is all the
more heartrending in that each is emotionally bonded to the
other: while Willy's love manifests itself in the form of an
unhealthy obsession, Biff's has progressed from adolescent
hero-worship to something far more profound, something
intangible based on his own growing self-awareness. To say
that their relationship is intense is an understatement. Built
into it, too, is a wider generational conflict; the world that
Willy has lived in is no longer possible; times have changed.
How is Biff to find a place for himself in this new world that
no one, certainly not his father, has prepared him for?
Willy, too, is perilously involved in a conflict with *his* father,
a man he has never known: witness his need to romanticise
substitute father-figures like his much older brother Ben and
the mythic salesman Dave Singleman.

Illusion, delusion and the madness of reality

Many of the key scenes in *Death of a Salesman* take place
inside Willy Loman's head. These are illusions, of course,
and as members of Miller's audience we experience them as
such. Yet they may be delusions, too, for some of them,
especially the scene when his sons plan to hang a hammock
in the backyard, may represent the past as Willy wants to
remember it, not as it actually was. His delusions in the real
world are of much greater concern; they have to do with his
exaggerations about himself and his overvaluation of his
sons. Yet for Willy the greatest madness of all is reality, the

world that has changed all round him. 'They don't know me any more,' he sighs in what may be his only instance of self-awareness in the entire play.

Growing old and growing up
Salesman is an unusual play in that it follows a double trajectory. On the one hand, and most significantly so, it shows the difficulty Biff faces, and the psychological obstacles he must overcome, as he tries to assert himself in reaching for his much-delayed maturity. But the play also demonstrates what it means to grow old in a culture that seems quite willing to pass you by, as Charley says in the Requiem, when 'you get yourself a couple of spots on your hat'. That's 'when they start not smiling back' and you know 'you're finished'.

The marginalised role of women
That *Salesman* represents a male-centred universe should be readily apparent. The women play predictable secondary parts, and that may be putting things mildly: there's an office secretary and worse to come, two call girls and The Woman caught in adultery. Not a very promising start. Linda, of course, is a far more complicated personality; as one of the four major protagonists, she is in fact the only fully developed female character on board. Initially assigned the satellite parts of wife and mother, she negotiates a great deal of dramatic space for herself when she confronts her sons, and it is she – and she alone – who commands the empty stage in the final moments of the play.

Masculinity in American culture
Props and properties in *Salesman* define a stereotypical masculine culture of athleticism, machines, muscles and brawn: football, basketball, baseball, carpentry, cars and 'women'. Willy disparages Charley because he doesn't know how to handle tools, and dismisses Charley's son Bernard

because he's a lot better at books than at sports. Biff deplores
the confinement of holding a steady office job, which he
interprets as more than a mild form of emasculation. He'd
much rather be out herding cattle, doing man's work.
Happy, who does work in an office (but only as one of two
assistants to the assistant), plays out his masculinist fantasies
by having meaningless sexual encounters with the wives of
his superiors; as he says, he can't help himself. Surely the
male figures in this play feel that their masculinity is
threatened, as they define it in such a circumscribed way.
Willy can't take the job offered by his only friend because he
would feel humiliated by it; but his greatest humiliation as a
'man' is that he can no longer earn a living.

The myth of the Far West and other dreams of leaving
Escape from the picayune existence of everyday life seems to
be much on everyone's mind in *Death of a Salesman*. Biff's
wandering has taken him to the prototypical American
landscape, the Far West, to which he longs to return. Happy
says he'd like to join Biff there – someday, but perhaps not
right now. Uncle Ben thought he was going off to Alaska a
long time ago, but ended up in Africa instead. He wanted
his brother to join him, and for a moment Willy was
tempted until Linda drew him back. And of course their
father, the flute-maker, was always on the move. Escape
routes seem to be a Loman family trait. Willy, in fact, has
two of them: one to his garden, the other to his past. Oddly
enough, it is Linda, the play's only significant female figure,
who seems firmly planted in the here and now.

Advertising and adversity
Miller's play is loaded with consumerist goods that are
always in need of repair. Things fall apart – refrigerators,
vacuum cleaners, cars, the roof – just when they're about to
be paid off. The world imagined here is perennially on the
installment plan. The Lomans bought a Hastings
refrigerator, clearly a lemon, because 'they got,' as Linda

said in the past, 'the biggest ads of any of them!' Years later
Willy seems to have forgotten this prophetic exchange when
he says, 'I told you we should've bought a well-advertised
machine. Charley bought a General Electric and it's twenty
years old and it's still good, that son-of-a bitch.' Miller
presents an America on the verge of a consumerist rampage
– tape recorders and other electronic gadgets loom large in
the not-too-distant future – where buyers are at the mercy of
ad-men, and where products are timed to break down so
that new and not necessarily improved ones can be
purchased. The Lomans' biggest consumer asset, bought on
time of course, is their out-of-date house. At the end of the
play the mortgage is finally paid off, but there's nobody at
home to live in it.

Characters

Willy Loman
Miller once described his lead character in *Salesman* as 'a
man trying to write his name on ice on a hot July day'.
The statement goes to the heart of the matter, for it reveals
the way in which this figure is meant to be both mundane
and metaphorical, localised and lyrical, eccentric and yet
at the same time hugely emblematic. A working man in his
sixties – Linda gives his age as sixty-three – he has been a
salesman all his life, but as he tells his brother Ben, 'I still
feel – kind of temporary about myself.' The large sample
cases he carries seem to be almost an extension of himself,
though oddly enough we never find out what is inside
them. While his father sold flutes and other items he made
with his own hands, Willy has no real connection to the
inventory he hawks – dry goods? We never know for sure.
What motivates Willy, instead, is the sales and the sales
pitch. And yet he has never been much of a success at
either; he has merely eked out a modest living and a
marginal existence, all the time exaggerating his take.
Everything he owns has been purchased on time. What he

loves to do most of all is work in his garden, though this
pastime conflicts with the image of himself he tries to
project as a social animal, cracking jokes, giving people a
few laughs, shaking hands with small-town dignitaries,
above all being popular and 'well liked' as he drives his car
up and down the New England 'territory'. He takes it for
granted that his wife loves him, that she is totally devoted
to his well-being, and that she will stand by him and up for
him no matter what happens during their married life. He
addresses his real attention and affection to his sons, most
especially and almost obsessively so to Biff. It is this golden
boy who will fulfil the unrealised dreams he has always had
for himself, or so he believes. He never understands the
psychological burden he places on his son until it is far
too late.

   In the play we meet Willy at the most perilous moment in
his career: things are falling apart. The trajectory moves
relentlessly downwards as he loses his job, the confidence he
once had in himself and, most perilously of all, his ability to
distinguish illusion from reality. Haunted by visions sited in
the past, Willy experiences them as part escape-mechanism,
part phantasmagoria, part painful reminder of the road not
taken. At the end of the play he will move into this illusory
world completely.

Linda

Linda is configured and sometimes even marginalised as
Willy's long-suffering wife, but the play doesn't quite work
unless we consider that she must be more than that, too.
Her status in the drama depends in part on our
understanding of the historical period in which she is
placed, a moment in post-war America when the
complementary roles of wife, mother and homemaker are
featured in popular magazines and in the popular
imagination as every woman's *sine qua non*. In his stage
directions Miller tells us that 'she more than loves' Willy,
'she admires him'. Nothing she does on stage challenges her
fixity and her loyalty, implying that she accepts the roles

assigned to her and even embraces them – though to
contemporary eyes this may seem like some sort of pre-
feminist nightmare.

Does she suspect her husband of infidelity? If so, she lets
her guard down only once, when, confused, she asks 'What
woman?' in the midst of a conversation that seems to be
heading elsewhere. Linda, however, outsizes her role at
those moments when she speaks up – and decisively so – as
if she perceives that the safety and frail security of her
sheltered world is being threatened. She is, for example, the
only character on stage who effectively counters her
brother-in-law's arguments for taking Willy off with him to
Africa, empowering Willy to offer his own defence for
establishing himself 'here', and she will let Ben know exactly
what she thinks of him when he spars unfairly with her son
(one can only imagine what his business scruples must be
like). More to the point, she is fierce and fearless in seeking
to protect her mate, even against Biff, knowing full well that
any self-awareness forced upon him at this late date would
be lethal. In this sense it could be argued that, like Kate
Keller in *All My Sons*, she knows everything, though she may
not yet be ready to accept the part she has played in
enabling Willy to construct the elaborate fantasies about
himself and the boys who still call him 'pal'. In the context
in which we discover her, boxed-in as she is as much by the
looming apartment houses as by the limitations of her
assignment to the secondary part, one wonders if she would
really have been any better off had she pierced through the
shell of mutual denial. As if to complicate matters, Miller
surrenders the stage to her in the final moments of the play,
providing her with an eloquent curtain speech. But just
what is going through her mind when she utters words like
'free' and 'clear' and must now confront the bleak future
awaiting her?

Biff

The much-favoured elder son in the Loman family, Biff has
been brought up to play the featured role in an elaborate

game of charades fated to end badly. That he peaked too
soon is only a part of the problem. A terrible thing has been
done to him by the father he loves only too well. For that
same father's love, in return, has always been conditional:
bring home prizes, throw the strongest athletic pass,
'borrow' whatever you need – construction supplies, a
football, a carton of basketballs, a suit that lands him in jail
for three months, a pen – and don't worry about taking
answers on a high-school maths exam from someone else,
even from the 'puny' Bernard, for you are a leader of men
because 'I say so'. Disillusion and demystification were
always waiting for him around the corner, but when he
meets them the encounter comes in the ugliest of ways:
discovering that the father he has been trying to please all
his young life, and whose authority he never even dreamed
of questioning, is nothing more than a common adulterer.
Everything he had been taught to depend on is suddenly
swept away. In a certain sense Biff makes the same mistake
Chris Keller does in *All My Sons*, never thinking of the man
who stands before him as a person in his own right, but only
as the larger-than-life figure who is his father. In the case of
Salesman, Willy has gone a long way to foster such
unsustainable hero-worship. Biff's rebellion after the shock
of his discovery – he is, after all, still an adolescent – takes
the form of anger, fear and above all, retribution: ruining
his life is the best way to get back at his father.

As the play begins Biff, now in his early thirties, has
returned to Brooklyn on one of his periodic visits, this time
determined to assert his freedom from the tyranny of his
dysfunctional family's false expectations and the weighty
burden of guilt that have kept him in check. His maturity
and self-awareness are long overdue. But this homecoming
is fraught with more pain than even he might have
imagined: his father has been trying to kill himself. His
freedom requires a heavy purchase, one that Biff is at first
reluctant to make: forcing his father to confront reality and
see his son for who he is and what he was always fated to
become.

Happy
All his life Happy has been in the shadow of his elder
brother, reluctant or simply incapable of asserting himself in
the strange chemistry of family dynamics. He carves out a
workable space for himself by dodging any formidable
challenge that comes his way. He doesn't resent his brother,
nor does he blame his father for putting him (at best) in
second place; he merely tries to stay out of their way, though
he will offer the occasional comment from the sideline when
their antagonism reaches a fever-pitch. Linda seems to have
given up on him completely, though it should be noted that
he is the child, however negligent, who has chosen to stay
behind, not run off to find himself in 'the Far West'. In the
scenes from the past, Happy sometimes tried to gain Willy's
attention – 'I'm losing weight, you notice, Pop?'; but when
he realised that this was never forthcoming, he simply gave
up on it. He seems to have bought into the family myth that
if Biff turns out well, he will too. Happy talks big, and in this
respect, as in several others, he may be the true inheritor of
Willy's public posture – minus, of course, the sinking anxiety
that goes along with it in his father's case.

The Woman
Though the fact that she is unnamed might suggest that she
plays a minor role in the play's trajectory, she is in fact the
principal device Miller uses to pierce through Biff's illusions
and extend his father's guilt, despair and disappointment (in
himself as well as in his son). She lives on in Willy's memory,
and she haunts him; but for Biff, who discovers her in his
father's hotel room in Boston, she will always be brutally
present in the guise of infidelity, a betrayal as much of his
mother as of himself.

Uncle Ben
Willy's brother always remains 'inside his head' even in
those scenes when his presence doesn't materialise on stage.
A figure who, on a narrative level, represents the road not

taken, he is on another level the mechanism for elevating the play above the here-and-now, bringing its full symbolic and psychological dimensions to light. Ben is the link to the father Willy has never known; but he also provides access to the material success that has always eluded him. Willy needs to romanticise both, just as he does in his monologue about Dave Singleman.

Charley

In contrast to the mysterious presence of Ben, Willy's neighbour Charley plays the choral role, attempting to bring him back to earth when dangerous reveries intrude. Some of them involve the hagiography surrounding Biff – he says that 'the jails are full of fearless characters' who steal items like six-by-tens from construction sites, and jests when everyone goes off to cheer the home boy on in a city-wide tournament. But the more threatening reveries are of a different sort; they have to do with Willy's misconception that he can succeed in business merely by being 'well-liked'. 'Who liked J.P. Morgan?' Charley interjects, piercing Willy's balloon. Throughout, he remains a loyal friend. And he bankrolls Willy when the chips are down.

Bernard

Charley's hardworking and conscientious son is the foil for the high-school football-hero who is Biff. Willy disparages him for studying, but nonetheless encourages his son to make use of him, for he can be helpful in passing answers on to him during exams. Like the other boys in the neighbourhood, Bernard is susceptible to the Lomans' charms, but in the end it is his deliberateness and commitment to the straight-and-narrow that wins the day. As the young lawyer he becomes, he is described in the text as '*a quiet, earnest, but self-assured young man*'.

Howard Wagner
Another son, this time the boss's, he has inherited and now runs the family business for which Willy has worked for many years. Unlike Bernard, he has obviously done nothing to gain this privileged position other than have the good luck to be born in the right place at the right time, something he does not seem to take into account. He likes the toys that come along with his status, most particularly his new tape-recorder. Howard is more contemptuous of Willy than sympathetic, for he seems to see him as a throwback to past inefficiencies, which he dismisses as no longer practical in an economy where 'business is business'. He may feel a little sorry for Willy, but not enough to prevent him from firing him.

Jenny
Charley's secretary, she has worked in his office for some time, and tries to elicit the adult Bernard's help when she sees that Willy is distressed in the outer hall.

Stanley, Miss Forsythe and Letta
Three figures who appear in the restaurant scene, where Willy is supposed to meet Biff and Happy, they play functional roles in the unravelling of what was supposed to be a celebratory dinner. Miss Forsythe is a quick pick-up for Happy, and Letta is the friend she calls to make up a foursome with Biff. Stanley's role as the waiter is more nuanced; he may or may not see through Happy's pose as big-time big-spender – the bill doesn't get paid in the end – and his tenderness to Willy, the father they leave behind, is in marked contrast to the behaviour of Willy's two grown sons.

Major productions

An iconic work like *Death of a Salesman* is naturally to be found in the repertory of theatre companies around the world. The play is appealing because it is at once concrete and full of mysterious suggestion – not to mention the fact that it contains in abundance one of the things the playwright said he wanted to be remembered for: 'Some good parts for actors'. Each time *Salesman* is staged, the drama reaches out to find new audiences, renewing itself in the process. Miller said he was at first surprised by the huge emotional pull of the story; but as he approached his eightieth year, he observed that he now realised that you had to make an audience 'feel before it can be made to think'.

That combination of reactions has been characteristic of the effect the play has had in its most successful interpretations. The world premiere on 10 February 1949 at the Morosco Theatre in New York is by this time the subject of legend. Directed by Elia Kazan on a famous multi-platform set designed by Jo Mielziner – a set that has left an indelible mark on the history of stage scenography – the production starred Lee J. Cobb in the pivotal role of Willy Loman. The actor was such a sensation in this part that for years afterwards it was impossible to imagine any other Willy Loman. A big, burly man who could look as crumpled on stage as off, Cobb was nonetheless a player with huge and unexpected resources of dignity and understated eloquence, all of which he brought to the play. Mildred Dunnock was cast as Linda; she wanted the part so badly that she kept coming back to the casting calls, even after she was told her demeanour was far too dignified for the role. It was perhaps her greatest professional success. Featuring Arthur Kennedy as Biff and Cameron Mitchell as Happy, the production itself was also a huge critical and box-office success. The play won a Pulitzer Prize, a Tony Award and, coming just two years after *All My Sons*, Miller's second award from the New York Drama Critics' Circle. Later that same year Kazan directed *Death of a Salesman* in London, with Paul Muni as Willy Loman.

Thirty years later Michael Rudman, then a young director at the National Theatre in London, mounted a forceful revival in the Lyttelton Theatre, casting the veteran

actor Warren Mitchell in the lead. The director wanted to
bring the work back to Miller's Jewish roots. The playwright
had been clear about not giving the Lomans a specific
ethnic identity; his aim was to tell a story not about *some*
Americans, but about *all* Americans. Besides, the drama of
working-class Jewish America had already been portrayed
with clarity and vigour by Clifford Odets, whose
Depression-era *Awake and Sing!* was the single most
important play presented in New York by the Group
Theatre in the 1930s. Rudman's set included minor details
– a Hebrew/English calendar, for example – in an attempt
to make a point, and Mitchell used East End inflections to
give his character the authenticity his director required.
This was certainly an imposition on the play, but it worked.
Though Miller was Jewish, his family was by no means
working-class. Rudman, however, was a close reader, and
he was perceptive in picking up on the rhythms of New
York speech, heavily inflected as it is with a syntax based on
the rich metaphorical flavour of Yiddish, the language the
large number of Eastern European Jews brought with them
to America: 'You can't eat an orange and throw the peel
away,' Willy tells Howard Wagner, ' – a man is not a piece
of fruit!' Willy also uses the ultimate New York Jewish
phrase paying homage to the departed: 'may he rest in
peace.'

Among those who saw the 1979 National Theatre
production was the American film actor Dustin Hoffman.
He remembered how much he had been impressed with the
taped version of *Salesman* prepared for American television
in the early 1950s (see below). Hoffman brought the
production to New York, then back to London, casting
himself in the role of Willy Loman. Hoffman said he had
been waiting all his life to play a part like this; when he
began his career as a young actor, ads for 'leading man'
never meant 'short' and 'ethnic'. His Willy Loman, like
Warren Mitchell's, could be both; but in order to
accommodate the part to Hoffman's physical stature, in this
interpretation Willy became a 'short' man instead of a 'fat'
one.

The play became susceptible to even more dynamic changes in 1983. As part of the cultural exchange accompanying the normalisation of diplomatic relations between the Chinese People's Republic and the United States during the Nixon administration, the playwright was invited to supervise a major production in Beijing. The play was to be presented at the People's Art Theatre in the translation by Ying Ruocheng, who played Willy Loman under his own direction. Miller wasn't convinced that a highly personal story about the cost of a defeated life in capitalist America would make any sense in a collectivist, communist society. But as 'Salesman' in Beijing, the book he did with his wife Inge Morath clearly illustrates, Willy Loman's story was experienced in China as a family tragedy created in its own national image.

The Chicago-based director Robert Falls prepared a fiftieth anniversary production of *Death of a Salesman* as early as 1997, substituting a double stage-revolve for the original's platform set, thereby making us rethink the play's sense of stage geography and stylised spatialisation. Two years later Falls's ambitious production for the Goodman Theatre settled in for a sold-out run at the Eugene O'Neill Theatre on Broadway. Brian Dennehy, a powerful Willy Loman for a new generation of theatregoers, earned one of this show's several Tony Awards.

Film and television

1952: Laszlo Benedict directs a film version of the play starring Frederic March as Willy; Mildred Dunnock as Linda; Kevin McCarthy as Biff; and Cameron Mitchell as Happy. March had been Lee J. Cobb's replacement in the original New York production, and later took the show on tour in the US. The film incorporates many of the acting choices made in the original Kazan stagings in London and New York.

1966: Lee J. Cobb stars as Willy Loman with Mildred Dunnock as Linda in Alex Segal's production for American television. The adaptation wins three Emmy Awards, and features the young actors George Segal as Biff and Gene Wilder as Bernard. This production offers documentary evidence of Cobb's and Dunnock's legendary performances in the roles of Willy and Linda Loman.

1966: Alan Cooke directs Rod Steiger as Willy Loman for the 'BBC Play of the Month'. Steiger was oddly cast in the role – the wrong physical and vocal type for Willy Loman – but the rest of the cast shed new light on the other main characters.

1984: The director Volker Schlondoff directs a new adaptation of *Death of a Salesman* for television. Dustin Hoffman reprises his stage role as Willy Loman and also serves as co-producer. With John Malkovich as Biff, Stephen Lang as Happy, Charles Durning as the Lomans' neighbour Charley, and the Canadian actress Kate Reid in an exceptionally fine and nuanced portrayal of Linda, the CBS broadcast is seen on one night by 25 million viewers. In Spain and other venues around the world, the film is also screened in movie houses. Despite the exceptional cast for this production, film editing never fully succeeded in capturing the spontaneity of the stage play's temporal fluidity.

Further Reading

Works by Miller

Arthur Miller: Plays, 6 vols. London: (vol. 1: *All My Sons, Death of a Salesman, The Crucible, A Memory of Two Mondays, A View from the Bridge*; vol. 2: *The Misfits, After the Fall, Incident at Vichy, The Price, Creation of the World, Playing for Time*; vol. 3: *The American Clock, The Archbishop's Ceiling, Two-Way Mirror*; vol. 4: *The Golden Years, The Man Who Had All the Luck, I Can't Remember Anything, Clara*; vol. 5: *The Last Yankee, The Ride Down Mount Morgan, Almost Everybody Wins*; vol. 6: *Broken Glass, Mr Peters' Connections, Resurrection Blues, Finishing the Picture*). Methuen, 1988–2009

All My Sons, with commentary and notes by Toby Zinman. London: Methuen Drama, 2010

The Crucible, with commentary and notes by Susan C.W. Abbotson. London: Methuen Drama, 2010

A View from the Bridge, with commentary and notes by Stephen Marino. London: Methuen Drama, 2010

Echoes Down the Corridor: Collected Essays 1944–2000, ed. Steven R. Centola. London: Methuen, 2000

'Salesman' in Beijing. London: Methuen 1984

The Theatre Essays of Arthur Miller, ed. Robert A. Martin. London: Methuen, 1994

Timebends: A Life. London: Methuen, 1987

Secondary reading

Bigsby, Christopher, *Arthur Miller: 1915-1962*. London: Weidenfeld & Nicolson, 2008

——, *Arthur Miller: A Critical Study*. Cambridge: Cambridge University Press, 2004

——, ed. *Arthur Miller and Company*. London: Methuen, 1990

——, ed. *The Cambridge Companion to Arthur Miller*. Cambridge: Cambridge University Press, 1997

Brater, Enoch, *Arthur Miller: A Playwright's Life and Works*. London: Thames and Hudson, 2005

———, ed. *Arthur Miller's America: Theater and Culture in a Time of Change*. Ann Arbor: University of Michigan Press, 2005

———, ed. *Arthur Miller's Global Theater: How an American Playwright Is Performed on Stages around the World*. Ann Arbor: University of Michigan Press, 2007.

Centola, Steve, *Arthur Miller in Conversation*. Dallas: Contemporary Research Associates, 1993

Gottfried, Martin, *Arthur Miller: His Life and Work*. Cambridge, MA: Da Capo Press, 2003

Gussow, Mel, *Conversations with Miller*. New York: Applause Theatre & Cinema Books, 2002

Koon, Helene Wickham, ed. *Twentieth-Century Interpretations of 'Death of a Salesman'*. Englewood Cliffs, NJ: Prentice-Hall, 1983

Martin, Robert A., ed. *Arthur Miller: New Perspectives*. Englewood Cliffs, NJ: Prentice-Hall, 1982

Murphy, Brenda, *Miller: Death of a Salesman*. Cambridge: Cambridge University Press, 1995

Roudané, Matthew C., ed. *Approaches to Teaching 'Death of a Salesman'*. New York: MLA, 1995

———, ed. *Conversations with Arthur Miller*. Jackson: University Press of Mississippi, 1987

Savran, David, *Communists, Cowboys and Queers: The Politics of Masculinity in the Plays of Arthur Miller and Tennessee Williams*. Minneapolis: University of Minnesota Press, 1992

Death of a Salesman

Certain Private Conversations
in Two Acts and a Requiem

Characters

Willy Loman
Linda
Biff
Happy
Bernard
The Woman
Charley
Uncle Ben
Howard Wagner
Jenny
Stanley
Miss Forsythe
Letta

The action takes place in Willy Loman's house and yard and in various places he visits in the New York and Boston of today.

Act One

A melody is heard, played upon a flute. It is small and fine, telling of grass and trees and the horizon. The curtain rises.

Before us is the Salesman's house. We are aware of towering, angular shapes behind it, surrounding it on all sides. Only the blue light of the sky falls upon the house and forestage; the surrounding area shows an angry glow of orange. As more light appears, we see a solid vault of apartment houses around the small, fragile-seeming home. An air of the dream clings to the place, a dream rising out of reality. The kitchen at center seems actual enough, for there is a kitchen table with three chairs, and a refrigerator. But no other fixtures are seen. At the back of the kitchen there is a draped entrance, which leads to the living-room. To the right of the kitchen, on a level raised two feet, is a bedroom furnished only with a brass bedstead and a straight chair. On a shelf over the bed a silver athletic trophy stands. A window opens onto the apartment house at the side.

Behind the kitchen, on a level raised six and a half feet, is the boys' bedroom, at present barely visible. Two beds are dimly seen, and at the back of the room a dormer window. (This bedroom is above the unseen living room.) At the left a stairway curves up to it from the kitchen.

*The entire setting is wholly or, in some places, partially transparent. The roof-line of the house is one-dimensional; under and over it we see the apartment buildings. Before the house lies an apron, curving beyond the forestage into the orchestra. This forward area serves as the back yard as well as the locale of all **Willy**'s imaginings and of his city scenes. Whenever the action is in the present the actors observe the imaginary wall-lines, entering the house only through its door at the left. But in the scenes of the past these boundaries are broken, and characters enter or leave a room by stepping 'through' a wall onto the forestage.*

From the right, **Willy Loman**, *the Salesman, enters, carrying two large sample cases. The flute plays on. He hears but is not aware of it. He is past sixty years of age, dressed quietly. Even as he crosses the stage to the doorway of the house, his exhaustion is apparent. He unlocks the door, comes into the kitchen, and thankfully lets his burden down, feeling the soreness of his palms. A word-sigh escapes his lips – it might be 'Oh,* *boy, oh, boy.' He closes the door, then carries his cases out into the living-room, through the draped kitchen doorway.*

Linda, *his wife, has stirred in her bed at the right. She gets out and puts on a robe, listening. Most often jovial, she has developed an iron repression of her exceptions to* **Willy**'s *behavior — she more than loves him, she admires him, as though his mercurial nature, his temper, his massive dreams and little cruelties, served her only as sharp reminders of the turbulent longings within him, longings which she shares but lacks the temperament to utter and follow to their end.*

Linda (*hearing* **Willy** *outside the bedroom, calls with some trepidation*) Willy!

Willy   It's all right. I came back.

Linda   Why? What happened? (*Slight pause.*) Did something happen, Willy?

Willy   No, nothing happened.

Linda   You didn't smash the car, did you?

Willy (*with casual irritation*)   I said nothing happened. Didn't you hear me?

Linda   Don't you feel well?

Willy   I'm tired to the death. (*The flute has faded away. He sits on the bed beside her, a little numb.*) I couldn't make it. I just couldn't make it, Linda.

Linda (*very carefully, delicately*)   Where were you all day? You look terrible.

Willy   I got as far as a little above Yonkers, I stopped for a cup of coffee. Maybe it was the coffee.

Linda   What?

Willy (*after a pause*)   I suddenly couldn't drive any more. The car kept going off onto the shoulder, y'know?

Linda (*helpfully*)   Oh. Maybe it was the steering again, I don't think Angelo knows the Studebaker.

Willy   No, it's me, it's me. Suddenly I realize I'm goin' sixty miles an hour and I don't remember the last five minutes. I'm – I can't seem to – keep my mind to it.

Linda   Maybe it's your glasses. You never went for your new glasses.

Willy   No, I see everything. I came back ten miles an hour. It took me nearly four hours from Yonkers.

Linda (*resigned*)   Well, you'll just have to take a rest, Willy, you can't continue this way.

Willy   I just got back from Florida.

Linda   But you didn't rest your mind. Your mind is overactive, and the mind is what counts, dear.

Willy   I'll start out in the morning. Maybe I'll feel better in the morning. (*She is taking off his shoes.*) These goddam arch supports are killing me.

Linda   Take an aspirin. Should I get you an aspirin? It'll soothe you.

Willy (*with wonder*)   I was driving along, you understand? And I was fine. I was even observing the scenery. You can imagine, me looking at scenery, on the road every week of my life. But it's so beautiful up there, Linda, the trees are so thick, and the sun is warm. I opened the windshield and just let the warm air bathe over me. And then all of a sudden I'm goin' off the road! I'm tellin' ya, I absolutely forgot I was driving. If I'd've gone the other way over the white line I might've killed somebody. So I went on again – and five minutes later I'm dreamin' again, and I nearly – (*He presses two fingers against his eyes.*) I have such thoughts, I have such strange thoughts.

Linda   Willy, dear. Talk to them again. There's no reason why you can't work in New York.

Willy   They don't need me in New York. I'm the New England man. I'm vital in New England.

Linda   But you're sixty years old. They can't expect you to keep traveling every week.

Willy   I'll have to send a wire to Portland, I'm supposed to see Brown and Morrison tomorrow morning at ten o'clock to show the line. Goddammit, I could sell them! (*He starts putting on his jacket.*)

Linda (*taking the jacket from him*)   Why don't you go down to the place tomorrow and tell Howard you've simply got to work in New York? You're too accommodating, dear.

Willy   If old man Wagner was alive I'd a been in charge of New York now! That man was a prince, he was a masterful man. But that boy of his, that Howard, he don't appreciate. When I went north the first time, the Wagner Company didn't know where New England was!

Linda   Why don't you tell those things to Howard, dear?

Willy (*encouraged*)   I will, I definitely will. Is there any cheese?

Linda   I'll make you a sandwich.

Willy   No, go to sleep. I'll take some milk. I'll be up right away. The boys in?

Linda   They're sleeping. Happy took Biff on a date tonight.

Willy (*interested*)   That so?

Linda   It was so nice to see them shaving together, one behind the other, in the bathroom. And going out together. You notice? The whole house smells of shaving lotion.

Willy   Figure it out. Work a lifetime to pay off a house. You finally own it, and there's nobody to live in it.

Linda   Well, dear, life is a casting off. It's always that way.

Willy   No, no, some people – some people accomplish something. Did Biff say anything after I went this morning?

Linda   You shouldn't have criticized him, Willy, especially after he just got off the train. You mustn't lose your temper with him.

Willy   When the hell did I lose my temper? I simply asked him if he was making any money. Is that a criticism?

Linda   But, dear, how could he make any money?

Willy (*worried and angered*)   There's such an undercurrent in him. He became a moody man. Did he apologize when I left this morning?

Linda   He was crestfallen, Willy. You know how he admires you. I think if he finds himself, then you'll both be happier and not fight any more.

Willy   How can he find himself on a farm? Is that a life? A farmhand? In the beginning, when he was young, I thought, well, a young man, it's good for him to tramp around, take a lot of different jobs. But it's more than ten years now and he has yet to make thirty-five dollars a week!

Linda   He's finding himself, Willy.

Willy   Not finding yourself at the age of thirty-four is a disgrace!

Linda   Shh!

Willy   The trouble is he's lazy, goddammit!

Linda   Willy, please!

Willy   Biff is a lazy bum!

Linda   They're sleeping. Get something to eat. Go on down.

Willy   Why did he come home? I would like to know what brought him home.

Linda   I don't know. I think he's still lost, Willy. I think he's very lost.

Willy   Biff Loman is lost. In the greatest country in the world a young man with such – personal attractiveness, gets lost. And such a hard worker. There's one thing about Biff – he's not lazy.

Linda   Never.

Willy (*with pity and resolve*)   I'll see him in the morning; I'll have a nice talk with him. I'll get him a job selling. He could be big in no time. My God! Remember how they used to follow him around in high school? When he smiled at one of them their faces lit up. When he walked down the street . . . (*He loses himself in reminiscences.*)

Linda (*trying to bring him out of it*)   Willy, dear, I got a new kind of American-type cheese today. It's whipped.

Willy   Why do you get American when I like Swiss?

Linda   I just thought you'd like a change –

Willy   I don't want a change! I want Swiss cheese. Why am I always being contradicted?

Linda (*with a covering laugh*)   I thought it would be a surprise.

Willy   Why don't you open a window in here, for God's sake?

Linda (*with infinite patience*)   They're all open, dear.

Willy   The way they boxed us in here. Bricks and windows, windows and bricks.

Linda   We should've bought the land next door.

Willy   The street is lined with cars. There's not a breath of fresh air in the neighborhood. The grass don't grow any more, you can't raise a carrot in the back yard. They should've had a law against apartment houses. Remember those two beautiful elm trees out there? When I and Biff hung the swing between them?

Linda   Yeah, like being a million miles from the city.

Willy   They should've arrested the builder for cutting those down. They massacred the neighborhood. (*Lost.*) More and more I think of those days, Linda. This time of year it was lilac and wisteria. And then the peonies would come out, and the daffodils. What fragrance in this room!

Linda   Well, after all, people had to move somewhere.

Willy No, there's more people now.

Linda   I don't think there's more people. I think –

Willy There's more people! That's what ruining this country! Population is getting out of control. The competition is maddening! Smell the stink from that apartment house! And another one on the other side . . . How can they whip cheese?

*On **Willy**'s last line, **Biff** and **Happy** raise themselves up in their beds, listening.*

Linda   Go down, try it. And be quiet.

Willy (*turning to **Linda**, guiltily*)   You're not worried about me, are you, sweetheart?

Biff   What's the matter?

Happy   Listen!

Linda   You've got too much on the ball to worry about.

Willy   You're my foundation and my support, Linda.

Linda   Just try to relax, dear. You make mountains out of molehills.

Willy   I won't fight with him any more. If he wants to go back to Texas, let him go.

Linda   He'll find his way.

Willy   Sure. Certain men just don't get started till later in life. Like Thomas Edison, I think. Or B.F. Goodrich. One of them was deaf. (*He starts for the bedroom doorway.*) I'll put my money on Biff.

Linda   And Willy – if it's warm Sunday we'll drive in the country. And we'll open the windshield, and take lunch.

Willy   No, the windshields don't open on the new cars.

Linda   But you opened it today.

Willy   Me? I didn't. (*He stops.*) Now isn't that peculiar! Isn't that a remarkable – (*He breaks off in amazement and fright as the flute is heard distantly.*)

Linda   What, darling?

Willy   That is the most remarkable thing.

Linda   What, dear?

Willy   I was thinking of the Chevvy. (*Slight pause.*) Nineteen twenty-eight . . . when I had that red Chevvy – (*Breaks off.*) That funny? I coulda sworn I was driving that Chevvy today.

Linda   Well, that's nothing. Something must've reminded you.

Willy   Remarkable. Ts. Remember those days? The way Biff used to Simonize that car? The dealer refused to believe there was eighty thousand miles on it. (*He shakes his head.*) Heh! (*To* **Linda**.) Close your eyes, I'll be right up. (*He walks out of the bedroom.*)

Happy (*to* **Biff**)   Jesus, maybe he smashed up the car again!

Linda (*calling after* **Willy**)   Be careful on the stairs, dear! The cheese is on the middle shelf! (*She turns, goes over to the bed, takes his jacket, and goes out of the bedroom.*)

Light has risen on the boys' room. Unseen, **Willy** *is heard talking to himself, 'Eighty thousand miles,' and a little laugh.* **Biff** *gets out of bed, comes downstage a bit, and stands attentively.* **Biff** *is two years older than his brother* **Happy**, *well built, but in these days bears a worn air and seems less self-assured. He has succeeded less, and his dreams are stronger and less acceptable than* **Happy**'s. **Happy** *is tall, powerfully made. Sexuality is like a visible color on him, or a scent that many women have discovered. He, like his brother, is lost, but in a different way, for he has never allowed himself to turn his face toward defeat and is thus more confused and hard-skinned, although seemingly more content.*

Happy (*getting out of bed*)   He's going to get his license taken away if he keeps that up. I'm getting nervous about him, y'know, Biff?

Biff   His eyes are going.

Happy   No, I've driven with him. He sees all right. He just doesn't keep his mind on it. I drove into the city with him last week. He stops at a green light and then it turns red and he goes. (*He laughs.*)

Biff   Maybe he's color-blind.

Happy   Pop? Why he's got the finest eye for color in the business. You know that.

Biff (*sitting down on his bed*)   I'm going to sleep.

Happy   You're not still sour on Dad, are you, Biff?

Biff   He's all right, I guess.

Willy (*underneath them, in the living-room*)   Yes, sir, eighty thousand miles – eighty-two thousand!

Biff   You smoking?

Happy (*holding out a pack of cigarettes*)   Want one?

Biff (*taking a cigarette*)   I can never sleep when I smell it.

Willy   What a simonizing job, heh!

Happy (*with deep sentiment*)   Funny, Biff, y'know? Us sleeping in here again? The old beds. (*He pats his bed affectionately.*) All the talk that went across those two beds, huh? Our whole lives.

Biff   Yeah. Lotta dreams and plans.

Happy (*with a deep and masculine laugh*)   About five hundred women would like to know what was said in this room.

They share a soft laugh.

Biff   Remember that big Betsy something – what the hell was her name – over on Bushwick Avenue?

Happy (*combing his hair*)   With the collie dog!

Biff   That's the one. I got you in there, remember?

Happy Yeah, that was my first time – I think. Boy, there was a pig! (*They laugh, almost crudely.*) You taught me everything I know about women. Don't forget that.

Biff I bet you forgot how bashful you used to be. Especially with girls.

Happy Oh, I still am, Biff.

Biff Oh, go on.

Happy I just control it, that's all. I think I got less bashful and you got more so. What happened, Biff? Where's the old humor, the old confidence? (*He shakes* **Biff**'s *knee.* **Biff** *gets up and moves restlessly about the room.*) What's the matter?

Biff Why does Dad mock me all the time?

Happy He's not mocking you, he –

Biff Everything I say there's a twist of mockery on his face. I can't get near him.

Happy He just wants you to make good, that's all. I wanted to talk to you about Dad for a long time, Biff. Something's happening to him. He – talks to himself.

Biff I noticed that this morning. But he always mumbled.

Happy But not so noticeable. It got so embarrassing I sent him to Florida. And you know something? Most of the time he's talking to you.

Biff What's he say about me?

Happy I can't make it out.

Biff What's he say about me?

Happy I think the fact that you're not settled, that you're still kind of up in the air . . .

Biff There's one or two other things depressing him, Happy.

Happy What do you mean?

Biff Never mind. Just don't lay it all to me.

Happy   But I think if you just got started – I mean – is there any future for you out there?

Biff   I tell ya, Hap, I don't know what the future is. I don't know – what I'm supposed to want.

Happy   What do you mean?

Biff   Well, I spent six or seven years after high school trying to work myself up. Shipping clerk, salesman, business of one kind or another. And it's a measly manner of existence. To get on that subway on the hot mornings in summer. To devote your whole life to keeping stock, or making phone calls, or selling or buying. To suffer fifty weeks of the year for the sake of a two-week vacation, when all you really desire is to be outdoors, with your shirt off. And always to have to get ahead of the next fella. And still – that's how you build a future.

Happy   Well, you really enjoy it on a farm? Are you content out there?

Biff (*with rising agitation*)   Hap, I've had twenty or thirty different kinds of jobs since I left home before the war, and it always turns out the same. I just realized it lately. In Nebraska when I herded cattle, and the Dakotas, and Arizona, and now in Texas. It's why I came home now, I guess, because I realized it. This farm I work on, it's spring there now, see? And they've got about fifteen new colts. There's nothing more inspiring or – beautiful than the sight of a mare and a new colt. And it's cool there now, see? Texas is cool now, and it's spring. And whenever spring comes to where I am, I suddenly get the feeling, my God, I'm not gettin' anywhere! What the hell am I doing, playing around with horses, twenty-eight dollars a week! I'm thirty-four years old, I oughta be makin' my future. That's when I come running home. And now, I get here, and I don't know what to do with myself. (*After a pause.*) I've always made a point of not wasting my life, and every time I come back here I know that all I've done is to waste my life.

Happy   You're a poet, you know that, Biff? You're a – you're an idealist!

Biff   No, I'm mixed up very bad. Maybe I oughta get married. Maybe I oughta get stuck into something. Maybe that's my trouble. I'm like a boy. I'm not married, I'm not in business, I just – I'm like a boy. Are you content, Hap? You're a success, aren't you? Are you content?

Happy   Hell, no!

Biff   Why? You're making money, aren't you?

Happy (*moving about with energy, expressiveness*)   All I can do now is wait for the merchandise manager to die. And suppose I get to be merchandise manager? He's a good friend of mine, and he just built a terrific estate on Long Island. And he lived there about two months and sold it, and now he's building another one. He can't enjoy it once it's finished. And I know that's just what I would do. I don't know what the hell I'm workin' for. Sometimes I sit in my apartment – all alone. And I think of the rent I'm paying. And it's crazy. But then, it's what I always wanted. My own apartment, a car, and plenty of women. And still, goddammit, I'm lonely.

Biff (*with enthusiasm*)   Listen, why don't you come out West with me?

Happy   You and I, heh?

Biff   Sure, maybe we could buy a ranch. Raise cattle, use our muscles. Men built like we are should be working out in the open.

Happy (*avidly*)   The Loman Brothers, heh?

Biff (*with vast affection*)   Sure, we'd be known all over the counties!

Happy (*enthralled*)   That's what I dream about, Biff. Sometimes I want to just rip my clothes off in the middle of the store and outbox that goddam merchandise manager. I mean I can outbox, outrun, and outlift anybody in that store, and I have to take orders from those common, petty sons-of-bitches till I can't stand it any more.

Biff   I'm tellin' you, kid, if you were with me I'd be happy out there.

Happy (*enthused*)   See, Biff, everybody around me is so false that I'm constantly lowering my ideals . . .

Biff   Baby, together we'd stand up for one another, we'd have someone to trust.

Happy   If I were around you –

Biff   Hap, the trouble is we weren't brought up to grub for money. I don't know how to do it.

Happy   Neither can I!

Biff   Then let's go!

Happy   The only thing is – what can you make out there?

Biff   But look at your friend. Builds an estate and then hasn't the peace of mind to live in it.

Happy   Yeah, but when he walks into the store the waves part in front of him. That's fifty-two thousand dollars a year coming through the revolving door, and I got more in my pinky finger than he's got in his head.

Biff   Yeah, but you just said –

Happy   I gotta show some of those pompous, self-important executives over there that Hap Loman can make the grade. I want to walk into the store the way he walks in. Then I'll go with you, Biff. We'll be together yet, I swear. But take those two we had tonight. Now weren't they gorgeous creatures?

Biff   Yeah, yeah, most gorgeous I've had in years.

Happy   I get that any time I want, Biff. Whenever I feel disgusted. The only trouble is, it gets like bowling or something. I just keep knockin' them over and it doesn't mean anything. You still run around a lot?

Biff   Naa. I'd like to find a girl – steady, somebody with substance.

Happy   That's what I long for.

Biff   Go on! You'd never come home.

Happy   I would! Somebody with character, with resistance! Like Mom, y'know? You're gonna call me a bastard when I tell you this. That girl Charlotte I was with tonight is engaged to be married in five weeks. (*He tries on his new hat.*)

Biff   No kiddin'!

Happy   Sure, the guy's in line for the vice-presidency of the store. I don't know what gets into me, maybe I just have an overdeveloped sense of competition or something, but I went and ruined her, and furthermore I can't get rid of her. And he's the third executive I've done that to. Isn't that a crummy characteristic? And to top it all, I go to their weddings! (*Indignantly, but laughing.*) Like I'm not supposed to take bribes. Manufacturers offer me a hundred-dollar bill now and then to throw an order their way. You know how honest I am, but it's like this girl, see. I hate myself for it. Because I don't want the girl, and, still, I take it and – I love it!

Biff   Let's go to sleep.

Happy   I guess we didn't settle anything, heh?

Biff   I just got one idea that I think I'm going to try.

Happy   What's that?

Biff   Remember Bill Oliver?

Happy   Sure, Oliver is very big now. You want to work for him again?

Biff   No, but when I quit he said something to me. He put his arm on my shoulder, and he said, 'Biff, if you ever need anything, come to me.'

Happy   I remember that. That sounds good.

Biff   I think I'll go to see him. If I could get ten thousand or even seven or eight thousand dollars I could buy a beautiful ranch.

Happy I bet he'd back you. 'Cause he thought highly of you, Biff. I mean, they all do. You're well liked, Biff. That's why I say to come back here, and we both have the apartment. And I'm tellin' you, Biff, any babe you want . . .

Biff No, with a ranch I could do the work I like and still be something. I just wonder though. I wonder if Oliver still thinks I stole that carton of basketballs.

Happy Oh, he probably forgot that long ago. It's almost ten years. You're too sensitive. Anyway, he didn't really fire you.

Biff Well, I think he was going to. I think that's why I quit. I was never sure whether he knew or not. I know he thought the world of me, though. I was the only one he'd let lock up the place.

Willy (*below*) You gotta wash the engine, Biff?

Happy Shh!

Biff *looks at* **Happy**, *who is gazing down, listening.* **Willy** *is mumbling in the parlor.*

Happy You hear that?

They listen. **Willy** *laughs warmly.*

Biff (*growing angry*) Doesn't he know Mom can hear that?

Willy Don't get your sweater dirty, Biff!

A look of pain crosses **Biff**'s *face.*

Happy Isn't that terrible? Don't leave again, will you? You'll find a job here. You gotta stick around. I don't know what to do about him, it's getting embarrassing.

Willy What a simonizing job!

Biff Mom's hearing that!

Willy No kiddin', Biff, you got a date? Wonderful!

Happy Go on to sleep. But talk to him in the morning, will you?

Biff (*reluctantly getting into bed*)   With her in the house. Brother!

Happy (*getting into bed*)   I wish you'd have a good talk with him.

The light on their room begins to fade.

Biff (*to himself in bed*)   That selfish, stupid . . .

Happy   Sh . . . Sleep, Biff.

Their light is out. Well before they have finished speaking, **Willy**'*s form is dimly seen below in the darkened kitchen. He opens the refrigerator, searches in there, and takes out a bottle of milk. The apartment houses are fading out, and the entire house and surroundings become covered with leaves. Music insinuates itself as the leaves appear.*

Willy   Just wanna be careful with those girls, Biff, that's all. Don't make any promises. No promises of any kind. Because a girl, y'know, they always believe what you tell 'em, and you're very young, Biff, you're too young to be talking seriously to girls.

Light rises on the kitchen. **Willy***, talking, shuts the refrigerator door and comes downstage to the kitchen table. He pours milk into a glass. He is totally immersed in himself, smiling faintly.*

Willy   Too young entirely, Biff. You want to watch your schooling first. Then when you're all set, there'll be plenty of girls for a boy like you. (*He smiles broadly at a kitchen chair.*) That so? The girls pay for you? (*He laughs.*) Boy, you must really be makin' a hit.

Willy *is gradually addressing – physically – a point offstage, speaking through the wall of the kitchen, and his voice has been rising in volume to that of a normal conversation.*

Willy   I been wondering why you polish the car so careful. Ha! Don't leave the hubcaps, boys. Get the chamois to the hubcaps. Happy, use newspaper on the windows, it's the easiest thing. Show him how to do it, Biff! You see, Happy? Pad it up, use it like a pad. That's it, that's it, good work. You're doin' all right, Hap. (*He pauses, then nods in approbation for a few seconds, then looks upward.*) Biff, first thing we gotta do when we get time is clip that big branch over the house. Afraid it's gonna fall in a storm and hit the roof. Tell you what. We get a rope and sling her around, and then we climb up there with a couple of saws and take her down. Soon as you finish the car, boys, I wanna see ya. I got a surprise for you, boys.

Biff (*offstage*)   Whatta ya got, Dad?

Willy   No, you finish first. Never leave a job till you're finished, remember that. (*Looking toward the 'big trees'.*) Biff, up in Albany I saw a beautiful hammock. I think I'll buy it next trip, and we'll hang it right between those two elms. Wouldn't that be something? Just swingin' there under those branches. Boy, that would be . . .

Young Biff *and* **Young Happy** *appear from the direction* **Willy** *was addressing.* **Happy** *carries rags and a pail of water.* **Biff**, *wearing a sweater with a block 'S', carries a football.*

Biff (*pointing in the direction of the car offstage*)   How's that, Pop, professional?

Willy   Terrific. Terrific job, boys. Good work, Biff.

Happy   Where's the surprise, Pop?

Willy   In the back seat of the car.

Happy   Boy! (*He runs off.*)

Biff   What is it, Dad? Tell me, what'd you buy?

Willy (*laughing, cuffs him*)   Never mind, something I want you to have.

Biff (*turns and starts off*)   What is it, Hap?

Happy (*offstage*)   It's a punching bag!

Biff   Oh, Pop!

Willy   It's got Gene Tunney's signature on it!

Happy *runs onstage with a punching bag.*

Biff   Gee, how'd you know we wanted a punching bag?

Willy   Well, it's the finest thing for the timing.

Happy (*lies down on his back and pedals with his feet*)   I'm losing weight, you notice, Pop?

Willy (*to* **Happy**)   Jumping rope is good too.

Biff   Did you see the new football I got?

Willy (*examining the ball*)   Where'd you get a new ball?

Biff   The coach told me to practice my passing.

Willy   That so? And he gave you the ball, heh?

Biff   Well, I borrowed it from the locker room. (*He laughs confidentially.*)

Willy (*laughing with him at the theft*)   I want you to return that.

Happy   I told you he wouldn't like it!

Biff (*angrily*)   Well, I'm bringing it back!

Willy (*stopping the incipient argument, to* **Happy**)   Sure, he's gotta practice with a regulation ball, doesn't he? (*To* **Biff**.) Coach'll probably congratulate you on your initiative!

Biff   Oh, he keeps congratulating my initiative all the time, Pop.

Willy   That's because he likes you. If somebody else took that ball there'd be an uproar. So what's the report, boys, what's the report?

Biff   Where'd you go this time, Dad? Gee we were lonesome for you.

Willy (*pleased, puts an arm around each boy and they come down to the apron*)   Lonesome, heh?

Biff   Missed you every minute.

Willy   Don't say? Tell you a secret, boys. Don't breathe it to a soul. Someday I'll have my own business, and I'll never have to leave home any more.

Happy   Like Uncle Charley, heh?

Willy   Bigger than Uncle Charley! Because Charley is not – liked. He's liked, but he's not – well liked.

Biff   Where'd you go this time, Dad?

Willy   Well, I got on the road, and I went north to Providence. Met the Mayor.

Biff   The Mayor of Providence!

Willy   He was sitting in the hotel lobby.

Biff   What'd he say?

Willy   He said, 'Morning!' And I said, 'You got a fine city here, Mayor.' And then he had coffee with me. And then I went to Waterbury. Waterbury is a fine city. Big clock city, the famous Waterbury clock. Sold a nice bill there. And then Boston – Boston is the cradle of the Revolution. A fine city. And a couple of other towns in Mass., and on to Portland and Bangor and straight home!

Biff   Gee, I'd love to go with you sometime, Dad.

Willy   Soon as summer comes.

Happy   Promise?

Willy   You and Hap and I, and I'll show you all the towns. America is full of beautiful towns and fine, upstanding people. And they know me, boys, they know me up and down New England. The finest people. And when I bring you fellas up, there'll be open sesame for all of us, 'cause one thing, boys: I have friends. I can park my car in any street in New England, and the cops protect it like their own. This summer, heh?

Biff *and* **Happy** (*together*)   Yeah! You bet!

Willy   We'll take our bathing suits.

Happy   We'll carry your bags, Pop!

Willy   Oh, won't that be something! Me comin' into the Boston stores with you boys carryin' my bags. What a sensation!

Biff *is prancing around, practicing passing the ball.*

Willy   You nervous, Biff, about the game?

Biff   Not if you're gonna be there.

Willy   What do they say about you in school, now that they made you captain?

Happy   There's a crowd of girls behind him every time the classes change.

Biff (*taking* **Willy**'*s hand*)   This Saturday, Pop, this Saturday, just for you, I'm going to break through for a touchdown.

Happy   You're supposed to pass.

Biff   I'm takin' one play for Pop. You watch me, Pop, and when I take off my helmet, that means I'm breakin' out. Then you watch me crash through that line!

Willy (*kisses* **Biff**)   Oh, wait'll I tell this in Boston!

Bernard *enters in knickers. He is younger than* **Biff**, *earnest and loyal, a worried boy.*

Bernard   Biff, where are you? You're supposed to study with me today.

Willy   Hey, looka Bernard. What're you lookin' so anemic about, Bernard?

Bernard   He's gotta study, Uncle Willy. He's got Regents next week.

Happy (*tauntingly, spinning* **Bernard** *around*)   Let's box, Bernard!

Bernard   Biff! (*He gets away from* **Happy**.) Listen, Biff, I heard Mr Birnbaum say that if you don't start studyin' math he's gonna flunk you, and you won't graduate. I heard him!

Willy   You better study with him, Biff. Go ahead now.

Bernard   I heard him!

Biff   Oh, Pop, you didn't see my sneakers! (*He holds up a foot for* **Willy** *to look at.*)

Willy   Hey, that's a beautiful job of printing!

Bernard (*wiping his glasses*)   Just because he printed University of Virginia on his sneakers doesn't mean they've got to graduate him, Uncle Willy!

Willy (*angrily*)   What're you talking about? With scholarships to three universities they're gonna flunk him?

Bernard   But I heard Mr Birnbaum say –

Willy   Don't be a pest, Bernard! (*To his boys.*) What an anemic!

Bernard   Okay, I'm waiting for you in my house, Biff.

Bernard *goes off. The* **Lomans** *laugh.*

Willy   Bernard is not well liked, is he?

Biff   He's liked, but he's not well liked.

Happy   That's right, Pop.

Willy   That's just what I mean. Bernard can get the best marks in school, y'understand, but when he gets out in the business world, y'understand, you are going to be five times ahead of him. That's why I thank Almighty God you're both built like Adonises. Because the man who makes an appearance in the business world, the man who creates personal interest, is the man who gets ahead. Be liked and you will never want. You take me, for instance. I never have to wait in line to see a buyer. 'Willy Loman is here!' That's all they have to know, and I go right through.

Biff   Did you knock them dead, Pop?

Willy   Knocked 'em cold in Providence, slaughtered 'em in Boston.

Happy (*on his back, pedaling again*)   I'm losing weight, you notice, Pop?

Linda *enters, as of old, a ribbon in her hair, carrying a basket of washing.*

Linda (*with youthful energy*)   Hello, dear!

Willy   Sweetheart!

Linda   How'd the Chevvy run?

Willy   Chevrolet, Linda, is the greatest car ever built. (*To the boys.*) Since when do you let your mother carry wash up the stairs?

Biff   Grab hold there, boy!

Happy   Where to, Mom?

Linda   Hang them up on the line. And you better go down to your friends, Biff. The cellar is full of boys. They don't know what to do with themselves.

Biff   Ah, when Pop comes home they can wait!

Willy (*laughs appreciatively*)   You better go down and tell them what to do, Biff.

Biff   I think I'll have them sweep out the furnace room.

Willy   Good work, Biff.

Biff (*goes through wall-line of kitchen to doorway at back and calls down*)   Fellas! Everybody sweep out the furnace room! I'll be right down!

Voices   All right! Okay, Biff.

Biff   George and Sam and Frank, come out back! We're hangin' up the wash! Come on, Hap, on the double! (*He and* **Happy** *carry out the basket.*)

Linda   The way they obey him!

Willy   Well, that's training, the training. I'm tellin' you, I was sellin' thousands and thousands, but I had to come home.

Linda   Oh, the whole block'll be at that game. Did you sell anything?

Willy   I did five hundred gross in Providence and seven hundred gross in Boston.

Linda   No! Wait a minute, I've got a pencil. (*She pulls pencil and paper out of her apron pocket.*) That makes your commission . . . Two hundred – my God! Two hundred and twelve dollars!

Willy   Well, I didn't figure it yet, but . . .

Linda   How much did you do?

Willy   Well, I – I did – about a hundred and eighty gross in Providence. Well, no – it came to roughly two hundred gross on the whole trip.

Linda (*without hesitation*)   Two hundred gross. That's . . . (*She figures.*)

Willy   The trouble was that three of the stores were half closed for inventory in Boston. Otherwise I woulda broke records.

Linda   Well, it makes seventy dollars and some pennies. That's very good.

Willy   What do we owe?

Linda   Well, on the first there's sixteen dollars on the refrigerator –

Willy   Why sixteen?

Linda   Well, the fan belt broke, so it was a dollar eighty.

Willy   But it's brand new.

Linda   Well, the man said that's the way it is. Till they work themselves in, y'know.

They move through the wall-line into the kitchen.

Willy   I hope we didn't get stuck on that machine.

Linda   They got the biggest ads of any of them!

Willy   I know, it's a fine machine. What else?

Linda   Well, there's nine-sixty for the washing machine. And for the vacuum cleaner there's three and a half due on the fifteenth. Then the roof, you got twenty-one dollars remaining.

Willy   It don't leak, does it?

Linda   No, they did a wonderful job. Then you owe Frank for the carburetor.

Willy   I'm not going to pay that man! That goddam Chevrolet, they ought to prohibit the manufacture of that car!

Linda   Well, you owe him three and a half. And odds and ends, comes to around a hundred and twenty dollars by the fifteenth.

Willy   A hundred and twenty dollars! My God, if business don't pick up I don't know what I'm gonna do!

Linda   Well, next week you'll do better.

Willy   Oh, I'll knock 'em dead next week. I'll go to Hartford. I'm very well liked in Hartford. You know, the trouble is, Linda, people don't seem to take to me.

They move onto the forestage.

Linda   Oh, don't be foolish.

Willy   I know it when I walk in. They seem to laugh at me.

Linda   Why? Why would they laugh at you? Don't talk that way, Willy.

Willy *moves to the edge of the stage.* **Linda** *goes into the kitchen and starts to darn stockings.*

Willy   I don't know the reason for it, but they just pass me by. I'm not noticed.

Linda   But you're doing wonderful, dear. You're making seventy to a hundred dollars a week.

Willy   But I gotta be at it ten, twelve hours a day. Other men I don't know – they do it easier. I don't know why – I can't stop myself – I talk too much. A man oughta come in with a few words. One thing about Charley. He's a man of few words, and they respect him.

Linda   You don't talk too much, you're just lively.

Willy (*smiling*)   Well, I figure, what the hell, life is short, a couple of jokes. (*To himself.*) I joke too much! *The smile goes.*

Linda   Why? You're –

Willy   I'm fat. I'm very – foolish to look at, Linda. I didn't tell you, but Christmas time I happened to be calling on F. H. Stewarts, and a salesman I know, as I was going in to see the buyer I heard him say something about – walrus. And I – I cracked him right across the face. I won't take that. I simply will not take that. But they do laugh at me. I know that.

Linda   Darling . . .

Willy   I gotta overcome it. I know I gotta overcome it. I'm not dressing to advantage, maybe.

Linda   Willy, darling, you're the handsomest man in the world –

Willy   Oh, no, Linda.

Linda   To me you are. (*Slight pause.*) The handsomest.

From the darkness is heard the laughter of a woman. **Willy** *doesn't turn to it, but it continues through* **Linda***'s lines.*

Linda   And the boys, Willy. Few men are idolized by their children the way you are.

Music is heard as behind a scrim, to the left of the house, **The Woman***, dimly seen, is dressing.*

Willy (*with great feeling*)   You're the best there is, Linda, you're a pal, you know that? On the road – on the road I want to grab you sometimes and just kiss the life outa you.

The laughter is loud now, and he moves into a brightening area at the left, where **The Woman** *has come from behind the scrim and is standing, putting on her hat, looking into a 'mirror' and laughing.*

Willy   'Cause I get so lonely – especially when business is bad and there's nobody to talk to. I get the feeling that I'll never sell anything again, that I won't make a living for you, or a business, a business for the boys. (*He talks through* **The**

Woman's *subsiding laughter.* **The Woman** *primps at the 'mirror'.*)
There's so much I want to make for –

The Woman   Me? You didn't make me, Willy. I picked you.

Willy (*pleased*)   You picked me?

The Woman (*who is quite proper-looking,* **Willy**'s *age*)   I did. I've
been sitting at that desk watching all the salesmen go by, day
in, day out. But you've got such a sense of humor, and we do
have such a good time together, don't we?

Willy   Sure, sure. (*He takes her in his arms.*) Why do you have to
go now?

The Woman   It's two o'clock . . .

Willy   No, come on in! (*He pulls her.*)

The Woman   . . . my sisters'll be scandalized. When'll you
be back?

Willy   Oh, two weeks about. Will you come up again?

The Woman   Sure thing. You do make me laugh. It's good
for me. (*She squeezes his arm, kisses him.*) And I think you're a
wonderful man.

Willy   You picked me, heh?

The Woman   Sure. Because you're so sweet. And such a
kidder.

Willy   Well, I'll see you next time I'm in Boston.

The Woman   I'll put you right through to the buyers.

Willy (*slapping her bottom*)   Right. Well, bottoms up!

The Woman (*slaps him gently and laughs*)   You just kill me,
Willy. (*He suddenly grabs her and kisses her roughly.*) You kill me.
And thanks for the stockings. I love a lot of stockings. Well,
good night.

Willy   Good night. And keep your pores open!

The Woman   Oh, Willy!

The Woman *bursts out laughing, and* **Linda***'s laughter blends in.*
The Woman *disappears into the dark. Now the area at the kitchen table brightens.* **Linda** *is sitting where she was at the kitchen table, but now is mending a pair of her silk stockings.*

Linda   You are, Willy. The handsomest man. You've got no reason to feel that –

Willy (*coming out of* **The Woman***'s dimming area and going over to* **Linda**)   I'll make it all up to you, Linda, I'll –

Linda   There's nothing to make up, dear. You're doing fine, better than –

Willy (*noticing her mending*)   What's that?

Linda   Just mending my stockings. They're so expensive –

Willy (*angrily, taking them from her*)   I won't have you mending stockings in this house! Now throw them out!

Linda *puts the stockings in her pocket.*

Bernard (*entering on the run*)   Where is he? If he doesn't study!

Willy (*moving to the forestage, with great agitation*)   You'll give him the answers!

Bernard   I do, but I can't on a Regents! That's a state exam! They're liable to arrest me!

Willy   Where is he? I'll whip him, I'll whip him!

Linda   And he'd better give back that football, Willy, it's not nice.

Willy   Biff! Where is he? Why is he taking everything?

Linda   He's too rough with the girls, Willy. All the mothers are afraid of him!

Willy   I'll whip him!

Bernard   He's driving the car without a license!

The Woman*'s laugh is heard.*

Willy   Shut up!

Linda   All the mothers –

Willy   Shut up!

Bernard (*backing quietly away and out*)   Mr Birnbaum says he's stuck up.

Willy   Get outa here!

Bernard   If he doesn't buckle down he'll flunk math! (*He goes off.*)

Linda   He's right, Willy, you've gotta –

Willy (*exploding at her*)   There's nothing the matter with him! You want him to be a worm like Bernard? He's got spirit, personality . . .

As he speaks, **Linda**, *almost in tears, exits into the living-room.* **Willy** *is alone in the kitchen, wilting and staring. The leaves are gone. It is night again, and the apartment houses look down from behind.*

Willy   Loaded with it. Loaded! What is he stealing? He's giving it back, isn't he? Why is he stealing? What did I tell him? I never in my life told him anything but decent things.

Happy *in pajamas has come down the stairs;* **Willy** *suddenly becomes aware of* **Happy**'s *presence.*

Happy   Let's go now, come on.

Willy (*sitting down at the kitchen table*)   Huh! Why did she have to wax the floors herself? Every time she waxes the floors she keels over. She knows that!

Happy   Shh! Take it easy. What brought you back tonight?

Willy   I got an awful scare. Nearly hit a kid in Yonkers. God! Why didn't I go to Alaska with my brother Ben that time! Ben! That man was a genius, that man was success incarnate! What a mistake! He begged me to go.

Happy   Well, there's no use in –

Willy   You guys! There was a man started with the clothes on his back and ended up with diamond mines!

Happy   Boy, someday I'd like to know how he did it.

Willy   What's the mystery? The man knew what he wanted and went out and got it! Walked into a jungle, and comes out, the age of twenty-one, and he's rich! The world is an oyster, but you don't crack it open on a mattress!

Happy   Pop, I told you I'm gonna retire you for life.

Willy   You'll retire me for life on seventy goddam dollars a week? And your women and your car and your apartment, and you'll retire me for life! Christ's sake, I couldn't get past Yonkers today! Where are you guys, where are you? The woods are burning! I can't drive a car!

Charley *has appeared in the doorway. He is a large man, slow of speech, laconic, immovable. In all he says, despite what he says, there is pity, and, now, trepidation. He has a robe over pajamas, slippers on his feet. He enters the kitchen.*

Charley   Everything all right?

Happy   Yeah, Charley, everything's . . .

Willy   What's the matter?

Charley   I heard some noise. I thought something happened. Can't we do something about the walls? You sneeze in here, and in my house hats blow off.

Happy   Let's go to bed, Dad. Come on.

Charley *signals to* **Happy** *to go.*

Willy   You go ahead, I'm not tired at the moment.

Happy (*to* **Willy**)   Take it easy, huh? (*He exits.*)

Willy   What're you doin' up?

Charley (*sitting down at the kitchen table opposite* **Willy**)   Couldn't sleep good. I had a heartburn.

Willy   Well, you don't know how to eat.

Charley   I eat with my mouth.

Willy   No, you're ignorant. You gotta know about vitamins and things like that.

Charley   Come on, let's shoot. Tire you out a little.

Willy (*hesitantly*)   All right. You got cards?

Charley (*taking a deck from his pocket*)   Yeah, I got them. Someplace. What is it with those vitamins?

Willy (*dealing*)   They build up your bones. Chemistry.

Charley   Yeah, but there's no bones in a heartburn.

Willy   What are you talkin' about? Do you know the first thing about it?

Charley   Don't get insulted.

Willy   Don't talk about something you don't know anything about.

They are playing. Pause.

Charley   What're you doin' home?

Willy   A little trouble with the car.

Charley   Oh. (*Pause.*) I'd like to take a trip to California.

Willy   Don't say.

Charley   You want a job?

Willy   I got a job, I told you that. (*After a slight pause.*) What the hell are you offering me a job for?

Charley   Don't get insulted.

Willy   Don't insult me.

Charley   I don't see no sense in it. You don't have to go on this way.

Willy   I got a good job. (*Slight pause.*) What do you keep comin' in here for?

Charley   You want me to go?

Willy (*after a pause, withering*)   I can't understand it. He's going back to Texas again. What the hell is that?

Charley   Let him go.

Willy   I got nothin' to give him, Charley, I'm clean, I'm clean.

Charley   He won't starve. None a them starve. Forget about him.

Willy   Then what have I got to remember?

Charley   You take it too hard. To hell with it. When a deposit bottle is broken you don't get your nickel back.

Willy   That's easy enough for you to say.

Charley   That ain't easy for me to say.

Willy   Did you see the ceiling I put up in the living-room?

Charley   Yeah, that's a piece of work. To put up a ceiling is a mystery to me. How do you do it?

Willy   What's the difference?

Charley   Well, talk about it.

Willy   You gonna put up a ceiling?

Charley   How could I put up a ceiling?

Willy   Then what the hell are you bothering me for?

Charley   You're insulted again.

Willy   A man who can't handle tools is not a man. You're disgusting.

Charley   Don't call me disgusting, Willy.

Uncle Ben, *carrying a valise and an umbrella, enters the forestage from around the right corner of the house. He is a stolid man, in his sixties, with a mustache and an authoritative air. He is utterly certain of his destiny, and there is an aura of far places about him. He enters exactly as* **Willy** *speaks.*

Willy   I'm getting awfully tired, Ben.

Ben's *music is heard.* **Ben** *looks around at everything.*

Charley   Good, keep playing; you'll sleep better. Did you call me Ben?

Ben *looks at his watch.*

Willy   That's funny. For a second there you reminded me of my brother Ben.

Ben   I only have a few minutes. (*He strolls, inspecting the place.* **Willy** *and* **Charley** *continue playing.*)

Charley   You never heard from him again, heh? Since that time?

Willy   Didn't Linda tell you? Couple of weeks ago we got a letter from his wife in Africa. He died.

Charley   That so.

Ben (*chuckling*)   So this is Brooklyn, eh?

Charley   Maybe you're in for some of his money.

Willy   Naa, he had seven sons. There's just one opportunity I had with that man . . .

Ben   I must make a train, William. There are several properties I'm looking at in Alaska.

Willy   Sure, sure! If I'd gone with him to Alaska that time, everything would've been totally different.

Charley   Go on, you'd froze to death up there.

Willy   What're you talking about?

Ben   Opportunity is tremendous in Alaska, William. Surprised you're not up there.

Willy   Sure, tremendous.

Charley   Heh?

Willy There was the only man I ever met who knew the answers.

Charley Who?

Ben How are you all?

Willy (*taking a pot, smiling*) Fine, fine.

Charley Pretty sharp tonight.

Ben Is Mother living with you?

Willy No, she died a long time ago.

Charley Who?

Ben That's too bad. Fine specimen of a lady, Mother.

Willy (*to* **Charley**) Heh!

Ben I'd hoped to see the old girl.

Charley Who died?

Ben Heard anything from Father, have you?

Willy (*unnerved*) What do you mean, who died?

Charley (*taking a pot*) What're you talkin' about?

Ben (*looking at his watch*) William, it's half-past eight!

Willy (*as though to dispel his confusion he angrily stops* **Charley**'s *hand*) That's my build!

Charley I put the ace –

Willy If you don't know how to play this game I'm not gonna throw my money away on you!

Charley (*rising*) It was my ace, for God's sake!

Willy I'm through, I'm through!

Ben When did Mother die?

Willy Long ago. Since the beginning you never knew how to play cards.

Charley (*picks up the cards and goes to the door*)   All right! Next time I'll bring a deck with five aces.

Willy   I don't play that kind of game!

Charley (*turning to him*)   You ought to be ashamed of yourself!

Willy   Yeah?

Charley   Yeah! (*He goes out.*)

Willy (*slamming the door after him*)   Ignoramus!

Ben (*as **Willy** comes toward him through the wall-line of the kitchen*) So you're William.

Willy (*shaking **Ben**'s hand*)   Ben! I've been waiting for you so long! What's the answer? How did you do it?

Ben   Oh, there's a story in that.

Linda *enters the forestage, as of old, carrying the wash basket.*

Linda   Is this Ben?

Ben (*gallantly*)   How do you do, my dear.

Linda   Where've you been all these years? Willy's always wondered why you –

Willy (*pulling **Ben** away from her impatiently*)   Where is Dad? Didn't you follow him? How did you get started?

Ben   Well, I don't know how much you remember.

Willy   Well, I was just a baby, of course, only three or four years old –

Ben   Three years and eleven months.

Willy   What a memory, Ben!

Ben   I have many enterprises, William, and I have never kept books.

Willy   I remember I was sitting under the wagon in – was it Nebraska?

Ben   It was South Dakota, and I gave you a bunch of wild flowers.

Willy   I remember you walking away down some open road.

Ben (*laughing*)   I was going to find Father in Alaska.

Willy   Where is he?

Ben   At that age I had a very faulty view of geography, William. I discovered after a few days that I was heading due south, so instead of Alaska, I ended up in Africa.

Linda   Africa!

Willy   The Gold Coast!

Ben   Principally diamond mines.

Linda   Diamond mines!

Ben   Yes, my dear. But I've only a few minutes –

Willy   No! Boys! Boys! (*Young* **Biff** *and* **Happy** *appear.*) Listen to this. This is your Uncle Ben, a great man! Tell my boys, Ben!

Ben   Why, boys, when I was seventeen I walked into the jungle, and when I was twenty-one I walked out. (*He laughs.*) And by God I was rich.

Willy (*to the boys*)   You see what I been talking about? The greatest things can happen!

Ben (*glancing at his watch*)   I have an appointment in Ketchikan Tuesday week.

Willy   No, Ben! Please tell about Dad. I want my boys to hear. I want them to know the kind of stock they spring from. All I remember is a man with a big beard, and I was in Mamma's lap, sitting around a fire, and some kind of high music.

Ben   His flute. He played the flute.

Willy   Sure, the flute, that's right!

New music is heard, a high, rollicking tune.

Ben   Father was a very great and a very wild-hearted man. We would start in Boston, and he'd toss the whole family into the wagon, and then he'd drive the team right across the country; through Ohio, and Indiana, Michigan, Illinois, and all the Western states. And we'd stop in the towns and sell the flutes that he'd made on the way. Great inventor, Father. With one gadget he made more in a week than a man like you could make in a lifetime.

Willy   That's just the way I'm bringing them up, Ben – rugged, well liked, all-around.

Ben   Yeah? (*To* **Biff**.) Hit that, boy – hard as you can. (*He pounds his stomach.*)

Biff   Oh, no, sir!

Ben (*taking boxing stance*)   Come on, get to me! (*He laughs.*)

Willy   Go to it, Biff! Go ahead, show him!

Biff   Okay! (*He cocks his fists and starts in.*)

Linda (*to* **Willy**)   Why must he fight, dear?

Ben (*sparring with* **Biff**)   Good boy! Good boy!

Willy   How's that, Ben, heh?

Happy   Give him the left, Biff!

Linda   Why are you fighting?

Ben   Good boy! (*Suddenly comes in, trips* **Biff**, *and stands over him, the point of his umbrella poised over* **Biff**'s *eye.*)

Linda   Look out, Biff!

Biff   Gee!

Ben (*patting* **Biff**'s *knee*)   Never fight fair with a stranger, boy. You'll never get out of the jungle that way. (*Taking* **Linda**'s *hand and bowing.*) It was an honor and a pleasure to meet you, Linda.

Linda (*withdrawing her hand coldly, frightened*)   Have a nice trip.

Ben (*to* **Willy**)   And good luck with your – what do you do?

Willy   Selling.

Ben   Yes. Well . . . (*He raises his hand in farewell to all.*)

Willy   No, Ben, I don't want you to think . . . (*He takes* **Ben**'s *arm to show him.*) It's Brooklyn, I know, but we hunt too.

Ben   Really, now.

Willy   Oh, sure, there's snakes and rabbits and – that's why I moved out here. Why, Biff can fell any one of these trees in no time! Boys! Go right over to where they're building the apartment house and get some sand. We're gonna rebuild the entire front stoop right now! Watch this, Ben!

Biff   Yes, sir! On the double, Hap!

Happy (*as he and* **Biff** *run off*)   I lost weight, Pop, you notice?

Charley *enters in knickers, even before the boys are gone.*

Charley   Listen, if they steal any more from that building the watchman'll put the cops on them!

Linda (*to* **Willy**)   Don't let Biff . . .

Ben *laughs lustily.*

Willy   You shoulda seen the lumber they brought home last week. At least a dozen six-by-tens worth all kinds a money.

Charley   Listen, if that watchman –

Willy   I gave them hell, understand. But I got a couple of fearless characters there.

Charley   Willy, the jails are full of fearless characters.

Ben (*clapping* **Willy** *on the back, with a laugh at* **Charley**)   And the stock exchange, friend!

Willy (*joining in* **Ben**'s *laughter*)   Where are the rest of your pants?

Charley   My wife bought them.

Willy   Now all you need is a golf club and you can go upstairs and go to sleep. (*To* **Ben**.) Great athlete! Between him and his son Bernard they can't hammer a nail!

Bernard (*rushing in*)   The watchman's chasing Biff!

Willy (*angrily*)   Shut up! He's not stealing anything!

Linda (*alarmed, hurrying off left*)   Where is he? Biff, dear! (*She exits.*)

Willy (*moving toward the left, away from* **Ben**)   There's nothing wrong. What's the matter with you?

Ben   Nervy boy. Good!

Willy (*laughing*)   Oh, nerves of iron, that Biff!

Charley   Don't know what it is. My New England man comes back and he's bleedin', they murdered him up there.

Willy   It's contacts, Charley, I got important contacts!

Charley (*sarcastically*)   Glad to hear it, Willy. Come in later, we'll shoot a little casino. I'll take some of your Portland money. (*He laughs at* **Willy** *and exits.*)

Willy (*turning to* **Ben**)   Business is bad, it's murderous. But not for me, of course.

Ben   I'll stop by on my way back to Africa.

Willy (*longingly*)   Can't you stay a few days? You're just what I need, Ben, because I – I have a fine position here, but I – well, Dad left when I was such a baby and I never had a chance to talk to him and I still feel – kind of temporary about myself.

Ben   I'll be late for my train.

They are at opposite ends of the stage.

Willy   Ben, my boys – can't we talk? They'd go into the jaws of hell for me, see, but I –

Ben   William, you're being first-rate with your boys. Outstanding, manly chaps!

Willy (*hanging on to his words*)   Oh, Ben, that's good to hear! Because sometimes I'm afraid that I'm not teaching them the right kind of – Ben, how should I teach them?

Ben (*giving great weight to each word, and with a certain vicious audacity*)   William, when I walked into the jungle, I was seventeen. When I walked out I was twenty-one. And, by God, I was rich! (*He goes out into darkness around the right corner of the house.*)

Willy   . . . was rich! That's just the spirit I want to imbue them with! To walk into a jungle! I was right! I was right! I was right!

Ben *is gone, but* **Willy** *is still speaking to him as* **Linda**, *in nightgown and robe, enters the kitchen, glances around for* **Willy**, *then goes to the door of the house, looks out and sees him. Comes down to his left. He looks at her.*

Linda   Willy, dear? Willy?

Willy   I was right!

Linda   Did you have some cheese? (*He can't answer.*) It's very late, darling. Come to bed, heh?

Willy (*looking straight up*)   Gotta break your neck to see a star in this yard.

Linda   You coming in?

Willy   Whatever happened to that diamond watch fob? Remember? When Ben came from Africa that time? Didn't he give me a watch fob with a diamond in it?

Linda   You pawned it, dear. Twelve, thirteen years ago. For Biff's radio correspondence course.

Willy   Gee, that was a beautiful thing. I'll take a walk.

Linda   But you're in your slippers.

Willy (*starting to go around the house at the left*)   I was right! I was! (*Half to* **Linda**, *as he goes, shaking his head.*) What a man! There was a man worth talking to. I was right!

Linda (*calling after* **Willy**)   But in your slippers, Willy!

Willy *is almost gone when* **Biff**, *in his pajamas, comes down the stairs and enters the kitchen.*

Biff   What is he doing out there?

Linda   Sh!

Biff   God Almighty, Mom, how long has he been doing this?

Linda   Don't, he'll hear you.

Biff   What the hell is the matter with him?

Linda   It'll pass by morning.

Biff   Shouldn't we do anything?

Linda   Oh, my dear, you should do a lot of things, but there's nothing to do, so go to sleep.

Happy *comes down the stair and sits on the steps.*

Happy   I never heard him so loud, Mom.

Linda   Well, come around more often; you'll hear him. (*She sits down at the table and mends the lining of* **Willy**'s *jacket.*)

Biff   Why didn't you ever write me about this, Mom?

Linda   How would I write to you? For over three months you had no address.

Biff   I was on the move. But you know I thought of you all the time. You know that, don't you, pal?

Linda   I know, dear, I know. But he likes to have a letter. Just to know that there's still a possibility for better things.

Biff   He's not like this all the time, is he?

Linda   It's when you come home he's always the worst.

Biff   When I come home?

Linda   When you write you're coming, he's all smiles, and talks about the future, and – he's just wonderful. And then the closer you seem to come, the more shaky he gets, and then, by the time you get here, he's arguing, and he seems angry at you. I think it's just that maybe he can't bring himself to – to open up to you. Why are you so hateful to each other? Why is that?

Biff (*evasively*)   I'm not hateful, Mom.

Linda   But you no sooner come in the door than you're fighting!

Biff   I don't know why. I mean to change. I'm tryin', Mom, you understand?

Linda   Are you home to stay now?

Biff   I don't know. I want to look around, see what's doin'.

Linda   Biff, you can't look around all your life, can you?

Biff   I just can't take hold, Mom. I can't take hold of some kind of a life.

Linda   Biff, a man is not a bird, to come and go with the springtime.

Biff   Your hair . . . (*He touches her hair.*) Your hair got so gray.

Linda   Oh, it's been gray since you were in high school. I just stopped dyeing it, that's all.

Biff   Dye it again, will ya? I don't want my pal looking old. (*He smiles.*)

Linda   You're such a boy! You think you can go away for a year and . . . You've got to get it into your head now that one day you'll knock on this door and there'll be strange people here.

Biff   What are you talking about? You're not even sixty, Mom.

Linda   But what about your father?

Biff (*lamely*)   Well, I meant him too.

Happy   He admires Pop.

Linda Biff, dear, if you don't have any feeling for him, then you can't have any feeling for me.

Biff Sure I can, Mom.

Linda No. You can't just come to see me, because I love him. (*With a threat, but only a threat, of tears.*) He's the dearest man in the world to me, and I won't have anyone making him feel unwanted and low and blue. You've got to make up your mind now, darling, there's no leeway any more. Either he's your father and you pay him that respect, or else you're not to come here. I know he's not easy to get along with – nobody knows that better than me – but . . .

Willy (*from the left, with a laugh*) Hey, hey, Biffo!

Biff (*starting to go out after* **Willy**) What the hell is the matter with him? (**Happy** *stops him.*)

Linda Don't – don't go near him!

Biff Stop making excuses for him! He always, always wiped the floor with you. Never had an ounce of respect for you.

Happy He's always had respect for –

Biff What the hell do you know about it?

Happy (*surlily*) Just don't call him crazy!

Biff He's got no character – Charley wouldn't do this. Not in his own house – spewing out that vomit from his mind.

Happy Charley never had to cope with what he's got to.

Biff People are worse off than Willy Loman. Believe me, I've seen them!

Linda Then make Charley your father, Biff. You can't do that, can you? I don't say he's a great man. Willy Loman never made a lot of money. His name was never in the paper. He's not the finest character that ever lived. But he's a human being, and a terrible thing is happening to him. So attention must be paid. He's not to be allowed to fall into his grave like an old dog. Attention, attention must be finally paid to such a person. You called him crazy –

Biff   I didn't mean –

Linda   No, a lot of people think he's lost his balance. But you don't have to be very smart to know what his trouble is. The man is exhausted.

Happy   Sure!

Linda   A small man can be just as exhausted as a great man. He works for a company thirty-six years this March, opens up unheard-of territories to their trademark, and now in his old age they take his salary away.

Happy (*indignantly*)   I didn't know that, Mom.

Linda   You never asked, my dear! Now that you get your spending money someplace else you don't trouble your mind with him.

Happy   But I gave you money last –

Linda   Christmas time, fifty dollars! To fix the hot water it cost ninety-seven fifty! For five weeks he's been on straight commission, like a beginner, an unknown!

Biff   Those ungrateful bastards!

Linda   Are they any worse than his sons? When he brought them business, when he was young, they were glad to see him. But now his old friends, the old buyers that loved him so and always found some order to hand him in a pinch – they're all dead, retired. He used to be able to make six, seven calls a day in Boston. Now he takes his valises out of the car and puts them back and takes them out again and he's exhausted. Instead of walking he talks now. He drives seven hundred miles, and when he gets there no one knows him any more, no one welcomes him. And what goes through a man's mind, driving seven hundred miles home without having earned a cent? Why shouldn't he talk to himself? Why? When he has to go to Charley and borrow fifty dollars a week and pretend to me that it's his pay? How long can that go on? How long? You

see what I'm sitting here and waiting for? And you tell me he
has no character? The man who never worked a day but for
your benefit? When does he get the medal for that? Is this
his reward – to turn around at the age of sixty-three and find
his sons, who he loved better than his life, one a philandering
bum –

Happy Mom!

Linda That's all you are, my baby! (*To* **Biff**.) And you! What
happened to the love you had for him? You were such pals!
How you used to talk to him on the phone every night! How
lonely he was till he could come home to you!

Biff All right, Mom. I'll live here in my room, and I'll get a
job. I'll keep away from him, that's all.

Linda No, Biff. You can't stay here and fight all the time.

Biff He threw me out of this house, remember that.

Linda Why did he do that? I never knew why.

Biff Because I know he's a fake and he doesn't like anybody
around who knows!

Linda Why a fake? In what way? What do you mean?

Biff Just don't lay it all at my feet. It's between me and him –
that's all I have to say. I'll chip in from now on. He'll settle for
half my pay check. He'll be all right. I'm going to bed. (*He
starts for the stairs.*)

Linda He won't be all right.

Biff (*turning on the stairs, furiously*) I hate this city and I'll stay
here. Now what do you want?

Linda He's dying, Biff.

Happy *turns quickly to her, shocked.*

Biff (*after a pause*) Why is he dying?

Linda He's been trying to kill himself.

Biff (*with great horror*) How?

Linda   I live from day to day.

Biff   What're you talking about?

Linda   Remember I wrote you that he smashed up the car again? In February?

Biff   Well?

Linda   The insurance inspector came. He said that they have evidence. That all these accidents in the last year – weren't – weren't – accidents.

Happy   How can they tell that? That's a lie.

Linda   It seems there's a woman . . . (*She takes a breath as:*)

Biff (*sharply but contained*)   What woman?

Linda (*simultaneously*)   . . . and this woman . . .

Linda   What?

Biff   Nothing. Go ahead.

Linda   What did you say?

Biff   Nothing. I just said what woman?

Happy   What about her?

Linda   Well, it seems she was walking down the road and saw his car. She says that he wasn't driving fast at all, and that he didn't skid. She says he came to that little bridge, and then deliberately smashed into the railing, and it was only the shallowness of the water that saved him.

Biff   Oh, no, he probably just fell asleep again.

Linda   I don't think he fell asleep.

Biff   Why not?

Linda   Last month . . . (*With great difficulty.*) Oh, boys, it's so hard to say a thing like this! He's just a big stupid man to you, but I tell you there's more good in him than in many other people. (*She chokes, wipes her eyes.*) I was looking for a fuse. The lights blew out, and I went down the cellar. And behind the fuse box – it happened to fall out – was a length of rubber pipe – just short.

Happy   No kidding?

Linda   There's a little attachment on the end of it. I knew right away. And sure enough, on the bottom of the water heater there's a new little nipple on the gas pipe.

Happy (*angrily*)   That – jerk.

Biff   Did you have it taken off?

Linda   I'm – I'm ashamed to. How can I mention it to him? Every day I go down and take away that little rubber pipe. But, when he comes home, I put it back where it was. How can I insult him that way? I don't know what to do. I live from day to day, boys. I tell you, I know every thought in his mind. It sounds so old-fashioned and silly, but I tell you he put his whole life into you and you've turned your backs on him. (*She is bent over in the chair, weeping, her face in her hands.*) Biff, I swear to God! Biff, his life is in your hands!

Happy (*to* **Biff**)   How do you like that damned fool!

Biff (*kissing her*)   All right, pal, all right. It's all settled now. I've been remiss. I know that, Mom. But now I'll stay, and I swear to you, I'll apply myself. (*Kneeling in front of her, in a fever of self-reproach.*) It's just – you see, Mom, I don't fit in business. Not that I won't try. I'll try, and I'll make good.

Happy   Sure you will. The trouble with you in business was you never tried to please people.

Biff   I know, I –

Happy   Like when you worked for Harrison's. Bob Harrison said you were tops, and then you go and do some damn fool thing like whistling whole songs in the elevator like a comedian.

Biff (*against* **Happy**)   So what? I like to whistle sometimes.

Happy   You don't raise a guy to a responsible job who whistles in the elevator!

Linda   Well, don't argue about it now.

Happy   Like when you'd go off and swim in the middle of the day instead of taking the line around.

Biff (*his resentment rising*)   Well, don't you run off? You take off sometimes, don't you? On a nice summer day?

Happy   Yeah, but I cover myself!

Linda   Boys!

Happy   If I'm going to take a fade the boss can call any number where I'm supposed to be and they'll swear to him that I just left. I'll tell you something that I hate to say, Biff, but in the business world some of them think you're crazy.

Biff (*angered*)   Screw the business world!

Happy   All right, screw it! Great, but cover yourself!

Linda   Hap, Hap!

Biff   I don't care what they think! They've laughed at Dad for years, and you know why? Because we don't belong in this nut house of a city! We should be mixing cement on some open plain, or – or carpenters. A carpenter is allowed to whistle!

Willy *walks in from the entrance of the house, at left.*

Willy   Even your grandfather was better than a carpenter. (*Pause. They watch him.*) You never grew up. Bernard does not whistle in the elevator, I assure you.

Biff (*as though to laugh* **Willy** *out of it*)   Yeah, but you do, Pop.

Willy   I never in my life whistled in an elevator! And who in the business world thinks I'm crazy?

Biff   I didn't mean it like that, Pop. Now don't make a whole thing out of it, will ya?

Willy   Go back to the West! Be a carpenter, a cowboy, enjoy yourself!

Linda   Willy, he was just saying –

Willy   I heard what he said!

Happy (*trying to quiet* **Willy**)   Hey, Pop, come on now . . .

Willy (*continuing over* **Happy**'*s line*)   They laugh at me, heh?
Go to Filene's, go to the Hub, go to Slattery's, Boston. Call out
the name Willy Loman and see what happens! Big shot!

Biff   All right, Pop.

Willy   Big!

Biff   All right!

Willy   Why do you always insult me?

Biff   I didn't say a word. (*To* **Linda**) Did I say a word?

Linda   He didn't say anything, Willy.

Willy (*going to the doorway of the living-room*)   All right, good
night, good night.

Linda   Willy, dear, he just decided . . .

Willy (*to* **Biff**)   If you get tired hanging around tomorrow,
paint the ceiling I put up in the living-room.

Biff   I'm leaving early tomorrow.

Happy   He's going to see Bill Oliver, Pop.

Willy (*interestedly*)   Oliver? For what?

Biff (*with reserve, but trying, trying*)   He always said he'd stake me.
I'd like to go into business, so maybe I can take him up on it.

Linda   Isn't that wonderful?

Willy   Don't interrupt. What's wonderful about it? There's
fifty men in the City of New York who'd stake him. (*To* **Biff**.)
Sporting goods?

Biff   I guess so. I know something about it and –

Willy   He knows something about it! You know sporting
goods better than Spalding, for God's sake! How much is he
giving you?

Biff   I don't know, I didn't even see him yet, but –

Willy   Then what're you talkin' about?

Biff (*getting angry*)   Well, all I said was I'm gonna see him, that's all!

Willy (*turning away*)   Ah, you're counting your chickens again.

Biff (*starting left for the stairs*)   Oh, Jesus, I'm going to sleep!

Willy (*calling after him*)   Don't curse in this house!

Biff (*turning*)   Since when did you get so clean?

Happy (*trying to stop them*)   Wait a . . .

Willy   Don't use that language to me! I won't have it!

Happy (*grabbing* **Biff**, *shouts*)   Wait a minute! I got an idea. I got a feasible idea. Come here, Biff, let's talk this over now, let's talk some sense here. When I was down in Florida last time, I thought of a great idea to sell sporting goods. It just came back to me. You and I, Biff – we have a line, the Loman Line. We train a couple of weeks, and put on a couple of exhibitions, see?

Willy   That's an idea!

Happy   Wait! We form two basketball teams, see? Two water-polo teams. We play each other. It's a million dollars' worth of publicity. Two brothers, see? The Loman Brothers. Displays in the Royal Palms – all the hotels. And banners over the ring and the basketball court: 'Loman Brothers.' Baby, we could sell sporting goods!

Willy   That is a one-million-dollar idea!

Linda   Marvelous!

Biff   I'm in great shape as far as that's concerned.

Happy   And the beauty of it is, Biff, it wouldn't be like a business. We'd be out playin' ball again . . .

Biff (*enthused*)   Yeah, that's . . .

Willy   Million-dollar . . .

Happy   And you wouldn't get fed up with it, Biff. It'd be the family again. There'd be the old honor, and comradeship, and if you wanted to go off for a swim or somethin' – well, you'd do it! Without some smart cooky gettin' up ahead of you!

Willy   Lick the world! You guys together could absolutely lick the civilized world.

Biff   I'll see Oliver tomorrow. Hap, if we could work that out . . .

Linda   Maybe things are beginning to –

Willy (*wildly enthused, to* **Linda**)   Stop interrupting! (*To* **Biff**.) But don't wear sport jacket and slacks when you see Oliver.

Biff   No, I'll –

Willy   A business suit, and talk as little as possible, and don't crack any jokes.

Biff   He did like me. Always liked me.

Linda   He loved you!

Willy (*to* **Linda**)   Will you stop! (*To* **Biff**.) Walk in very serious. You are not applying for a boy's job. Money is to pass. Be quiet, fine, and serious. Everybody likes a kidder, but nobody lends him money.

Happy   I'll try to get some myself, Biff. I'm sure I can.

Willy   I see great things for you kids, I think your troubles are over. But remember, start big and you'll end big. Ask for fifteen. How much you gonna ask for?

Biff   Gee, I don't know –

Willy   And don't say 'Gee'. 'Gee' is a boy's word. A man walking in for fifteen thousand dollars does not say 'Gee'!

Biff   Ten, I think, would be top though.

Willy   Don't be so modest. You always started too low. Walk in with a big laugh. Don't look worried. Start off with a couple of your good stories to lighten things up. It's not what you say, it's how you say it – because personality always wins the day.

Linda   Oliver always thought the highest of him –

Willy   Will you let me talk?

Biff   Don't yell at her, Pop, will ya?

Willy (*angrily*)   I was talking, wasn't I?

Biff   I don't like you yelling at her all the time, and I'm tellin' you, that's all.

Willy   What're you, takin' over this house?

Linda   Willy –

Willy (*turning on her*)   Don't take his side all the time, goddammit!

Biff (*furiously*)   Stop yelling at her!

Willy (*suddenly pulling on his cheek, beaten down, guilt ridden*)   Give my best to Bill Oliver – he may remember me. (*He exits through the living-room doorway.*)

Linda (*her voice subdued*)   What'd you have to start that for? (**Biff** *turns away.*) You see how sweet he was as soon as you talked hopefully? (*She goes over to* **Biff**.) Come up and say good night to him. Don't let him go to bed that way.

Happy   Come on, Biff, let's buck him up.

Linda   Please, dear. Just say good night. It takes so little to make him happy. Come. (*She goes through the living-room doorway, calling upstairs from within the living-room.*) Your pajamas are hanging in the bathroom, Willy!

Happy (*looking toward where* **Linda** *went out*)   What a woman! They broke the mold when they made her. You know that, Biff?

Biff   He's off salary. My God, working on commission!

Happy   Well, let's face it: he's no hot-shot selling man. Except that sometimes, you have to admit, he's a sweet personality.

Biff (*deciding*)   Lend me ten bucks, will ya? I want to buy some new ties.

Happy   I'll take you to a place I know. Beautiful stuff. Wear one of my striped shirts tomorrow.

Biff   She got gray. Mom got awful old. Gee, I'm gonna go in to Oliver tomorrow and knock him for a –

Happy   Come on up. Tell that to Dad. Let's give him a whirl. Come on.

Biff (*steamed up*)   You know, with ten thousand bucks, boy!

Happy (*as they go into the living-room*)   That's the talk, Biff, that's the first time I've heard the old confidence out of you! (*From within the living-room, fading off.*) You're gonna live with me, kid, and any babe you want just say the word . . . (*The last lines are hardly heard. They are mounting the stairs to their parents' bedroom.*)

Linda (*entering her bedroom and addressing* **Willy**, *who is in the bathroom. She is straightening the bed for him*)   Can you do anything about the shower? It drips.

Willy (*from the bathroom*)   All of a sudden everything falls to pieces! Goddam plumbing, oughta be sued, those people. I hardly finished putting it in and the thing . . . (*His words rumble off.*)

Linda   I'm just wondering if Oliver will remember him. You think he might?

Willy (*coming out of the bathroom in his pajamas*)   Remember him? What's the matter with you, you crazy? If he'd've stayed with Oliver he'd be on top by now! Wait'll Oliver gets a look at him. You don't know the average caliber any more. The average young man today – (*He is getting into bed.*) is got a caliber of zero. Greatest thing in the world for him was to bum around.

Biff and **Happy** *enter the bedroom. Slight pause.*

Willy (*stops short, looking at* **Biff**)   Glad to hear it, boy.

Happy   He wanted to say good night to you, sport.

Willy (*to* **Biff**)   Yeah. Knock him dead, boy. What'd you want to tell me?

Biff   Just take it easy, Pop. Good night. (*He turns to go.*)

Willy (*unable to resist*)   And if anything falls off the desk while you're talking to him – like a package or something – don't you pick it up. They have office boys for that.

Linda   I'll make a big breakfast –

Willy   Will you let me finish? (*To* **Biff**.) Tell him you were in the business in the West. Not farm work.

Biff   All right, Dad.

Linda   I think everything –

Willy (*going right through her speech*)   And don't undersell yourself. No less than fifteen thousand dollars.

Biff (*unable to bear him*)   Okay. Good night, Mom. (*He starts moving.*)

Willy   Because you got a greatness in you, Biff, remember that. You got all kinds a greatness . . . (*He lies back, exhausted.* **Biff** *walks out.*)

Linda (*calling after* **Biff**)   Sleep well, darling!

Happy   I'm gonna get married, Mom. I wanted to tell you.

Linda   Go to sleep, dear.

Happy (*going*)   I just wanted to tell you.

Willy   Keep up the good work. (**Happy** *exits.*) God . . . remember that Ebbets Field game? The championship of the city?

Linda   Just rest. Should I sing to you?

Willy   Yeah. Sing to me. (**Linda** *hums a soft lullaby.*) When that team came out – he was the tallest, remember?

Linda   Oh, yes. And in gold.

Biff *enters the darkened kitchen, takes a cigarette, and leaves the house. He comes downstage into a golden pool of light. He smokes, staring at the night.*

Willy   Like a young god. Hercules – something like that. And the sun, the sun all around him. Remember how he waved to me? Right up from the field, with the representatives of three colleges standing by? And the buyers I brought, and the cheers when he came out – Loman, Loman, Loman! God Almighty, he'll be great yet. A star like that, magnificent, can never really fade away!

The light on **Willy** *is fading. The gas heater begins to glow through the kitchen wall, near the stairs, a blue flame beneath red coils.*

Linda (*timidly*)   Willy dear, what has he got against you?

Willy   I'm so tired. Don't talk any more.

Biff *slowly returns to the kitchen. He stops, stares toward the heater.*

Linda   Will you ask Howard to let you work in New York?

Willy   First thing in the morning. Everything'll be all right.

Biff *reaches behind the heater and draws out a length of rubber tubing. He is horrified and turns his head toward* **Willy**'s *room, still dimly lit, from which the strains of* **Linda**'s *desperate but monotonous humming rise.*

Willy (*staring through the window into the moonlight*)   Gee, look at the moon moving between the buildings!

Biff *wraps the tubing around his hand and quickly goes up the stairs.*

Curtain.

Act Two

Music is heard, gay and bright. The curtain rises as the music fades away. **Willy,** *in shirt sleeves, is sitting at the kitchen table, sipping coffee, his hat in his lap.* **Linda** *is filling his cup when she can.*

Willy   Wonderful coffee. Meal in itself.

Linda   Can I make you some eggs?

Willy   No. Take a breath.

Linda   You look so rested, dear.

Willy   I slept like a dead one. First time in months. Imagine, sleeping till ten on a Tuesday morning. Boys left nice and early, heh?

Linda   They were out of here by eight o'clock.

Willy   Good work!

Linda   It was so thrilling to see them leaving together. I can't get over the shaving lotion in this house!

Willy (*smiling*)   Mmm –

Linda   Biff was very changed this morning. His whole attitude seemed to be hopeful. He couldn't wait to get downtown to see Oliver.

Willy   He's heading for a change. There's no question, there simply are certain men that take longer to get solidified. How did he dress?

Linda   His blue suit. He's so handsome in that suit. He could be anything in that suit!

Willy *gets up from the table.* **Linda** *holds his jacket for him.*

Willy   There's no question, no question at all. Gee, on the way home tonight I'd like to buy some seeds.

Linda (*laughing*)   That'd be wonderful. But not enough sun gets back there. Nothing'll grow any more.

Willy   You wait, kid, before it's all over we're gonna get a little place out in the country, and I'll raise some vegetables, a couple of chickens . . .

Linda   You'll do it yet, dear.

Willy *walks out of his jacket.* **Linda** *follows him.*

Willy   And they'll get married, and come for a weekend. I'd build a little guest house. 'Cause I got so many fine tools, all I'd need would be a little lumber and some peace of mind.

Linda (*joyfully*)   I sewed the lining . . .

Willy   I could build two guest houses, so they'd both come. Did he decide how much he's going to ask Oliver for?

Linda (*getting him into the jacket*)   He didn't mention it, but I imagine ten or fifteen thousand. You going to talk to Howard today?

Willy   Yeah. I'll put it to him straight and simple. He'll just have to take me off the road.

Linda   And Willy, don't forget to ask for a little advance, because we've got the insurance premium. It's the grace period now.

Willy   That's a hundred . . . ?

Linda   A hundred and eight, sixty-eight. Because we're a little short again.

Willy   Why are we short?

Linda   Well, you had the motor job on the car . . .

Willy   That goddam Studebaker!

Linda   And you got one more payment on the refrigerator . . .

Willy   But it just broke again!

Linda   Well, it's old, dear.

Willy   I told you we should've bought a well-advertised machine. Charley bought a General Electric and it's twenty years old and it's still good, that son-of-a-bitch.

Linda   But, Willy –

Willy   Whoever heard of a Hastings refrigerator? Once in my life I would like to own something outright before it's broken! I'm always in a race with the junkyard! I just finished paying for the car and it's on its last legs. The refrigerator consumes belts like a goddam maniac. They time those things. They time them so when you finally paid for them, they're used up.

Linda (*buttoning up his jacket as he unbuttons it*)   All told, about two hundred dollars would carry us, dear. But that includes the last payment on the mortgage. After this payment, Willy, the house belongs to us.

Willy   It's twenty-five years!

Linda   Biff was nine years old when we bought it.

Willy   Well, that's a great thing. To weather a twenty-five year mortgage is –

Linda   It's an accomplishment.

Willy   All the cement, the lumber, the reconstruction I put in this house! There ain't a crack to be found in it any more.

Linda   Well, it served its purpose.

Willy   What purpose? Some stranger'll come along, move in, and that's that. If only Biff would take this house, and raise a family . . . (*He starts to go.*) Good-bye, I'm late.

Linda (*suddenly remembering*)   Oh, I forgot! You're supposed to meet them for dinner.

Willy   Me?

Linda   At Frank's Chop House on Forty-eighth near Sixth Avenue –

Willy   Is that so! How about you?

Linda   No, just the three of you. They're gonna blow you to a big meal!

Willy   Don't say! Who thought of that?

Linda   Biff came to me this morning, Willy, and he said, 'Tell Dad, we want to blow him to a big meal.' Be there six o'clock. You and your two boys are going to have dinner.

Willy   Gee whiz! That's really somethin'. I'm gonna knock Howard for a loop, kid. I'll get an advance, and I'll come home with a New York job. Goddammit, now I'm gonna do it!

Linda   Oh, that's the spirit, Willy!

Willy   I will never get behind a wheel the rest of my life!

Linda   It's changing, Willy, I can feel it changing!

Willy   Beyond a question. G'by, I'm late. (*He starts to go again.*)

Linda (*calling after him as she runs to the kitchen table for a handkerchief*)   You got your glasses?

Willy (*feels for them, then comes back in*)   Yeah, yeah, got my glasses.

Linda (*giving him the handkerchief*)   And a handkerchief.

Willy   Yeah, handkerchief.

Linda   And your saccharine?

Willy   Yeah, my saccharine.

Linda   Be careful on the subway stairs.

She kisses him, and a silk stocking is seen hanging from her hand. **Willy** *notices it.*

Willy   Will you stop mending stockings? At least while I'm in the house. It gets me nervous. I can't tell you. Please.

Linda *hides the stocking in her hand as she follows* **Willy** *across the forestage in front of the house.*

Linda   Remember, Frank's Chop House.

Willy (*passing the apron*)   Maybe beets would grow out there.

Linda (*laughing*)   But you tried so many times.

Willy   Yeah. Well, don't work hard today. (*He disappears around the right corner of the house.*)

Linda   Be careful!

As **Willy** *vanishes,* **Linda** *waves to him. Suddenly the phone rings. She runs across the stage and into the kitchen and lifts it.*

Linda   Hello? Oh, Biff! I'm so glad you called, I just . . . Yes, sure, I just told him. Yes, he'll be there for dinner at six o'clock, I didn't forget. Listen, I was just dying to tell you. You know that little rubber pipe I told you about? That he connected to the gas heater? I finally decided to go down the cellar this morning and take it away and destroy it. But it's gone! Imagine? He took it away himself, it isn't there! (*She listens.*) When? Oh, then you took it. Oh – nothing, it's just that I'd hoped he'd taken it away himself. Oh, I'm not worried, darling, because this morning he left in such high spirits, it was like the old days! I'm not afraid any more. Did Mr Oliver see you? . . . Well, you wait there then. And make a nice impression on him, darling. Just don't perspire too much before you see him. And have a nice time with Dad. He may have big news too! . . . That's right, a New York job. And be sweet to him tonight, dear. Be loving to him. Because he's only a little boat looking for a harbor. (*She is trembling with sorrow and joy.*) Oh, that's wonderful, Biff, you'll save his life. Thanks, darling. Just put your arm around him when he comes into the restaurant. Give him a smile. That's the boy . . . Good-bye, dear . . . You got your comb? . . . That's fine. Good-bye, Biff dear.

In the middle of her speech, **Howard Wagner**, *thirty-six, wheels on a small typewriter table on which is a wire-recording machine and proceeds to plug it in. This is on the left forestage. Light slowly fades on* **Linda** *as it rises on* **Howard**. **Howard** *is intent on threading the machine and only glances over his shoulder as* **Willy** *appears.*

Willy   Pst! Pst!

Howard   Hello, Willy, come in.

Willy   Like to have a little talk with you, Howard.

Howard   Sorry to keep you waiting. I'll be with you in a minute.

Willy   What's that, Howard?

Howard   Didn't you ever see one of these? Wire recorder.

Willy   Oh. Can we talk a minute?

Howard   Records things. Just got delivery yesterday. Been driving me crazy, the most terrific machine I ever saw in my life. I was up all night with it.

Willy   What do you do with it?

Howard   I bought it for dictation, but you can do anything with it. Listen to this. I had it home last night. Listen to what I picked up. The first one is my daughter. Get this. (*He flicks the switch and 'Roll out the Barrel' is heard being whistled.*) Listen to that kid whistle.

Willy   That is lifelike, isn't it?

Howard   Seven years old. Get that tone.

Willy   Ts, ts. Like to ask a little favor if you . . .

The whistling breaks off, and the voice of **Howard***'s daughter is heard.*

His Daughter   'Now you, Daddy.'

Howard   She's crazy for me! (*Again the same song is whistled.*) That's me! Ha! (*He winks.*)

Willy   You're very good!

The whistling breaks off again. The machine runs silent for a moment.

Howard   Sh! Get this now, this is my son.

His Son   'The capital of Alabama is Montgomery; the capital of Arizona is Phoenix; the capital of Arkansas is Little Rock; the capital of California is Sacramento . . .' (*And on, and on.*)

Howard (*holding up five fingers*)   Five years old, Willy!

Willy   He'll make an announcer some day!

His Son (*continuing*)   'The capital . . .'

Howard   Get that – alphabetical order! (*The machine breaks off suddenly.*) Wait a minute. The maid kicked the plug out.

Willy   It certainly is a –

Howard   Sh, for God's sake!

His Son   'It's nine o'clock, Bulova watch time. So I have to go to sleep.'

Willy   That really is –

Howard   Wait a minute! The next is my wife.

They wait.

Howard's Voice   'Go on, say something.' (*Pause.*) 'Well, you gonna talk?'

His Wife   'I can't think of anything.'

Howard's Voice   'Well, talk – it's turning.'

His Wife (*shyly, beaten*)   'Hello.' (*Silence.*) 'Oh, Howard, I can't talk into this . . .'

Howard (*snapping the machine off*)   That was my wife.

Willy   That is a wonderful machine. Can we –

Howard   I tell you, Willy, I'm gonna take my camera, and my bandsaw, and all my hobbies, and out they go. This is the most fascinating relaxation I ever found.

Willy   I think I'll get one myself.

Howard   Sure, they're only a hundred and a half. You can't do without it. Supposing you wanna hear Jack Benny, see? But you can't be at home at that hour. So you tell the maid to turn the radio on when Jack Benny comes on, and this automatically goes on with the radio . . .

Willy   And when you come home you . . .

Howard   You can come home twelve o'clock, one o'clock, any time you like, and you get yourself a Coke and sit yourself down, throw the switch, and there's Jack Benny's program in the middle of the night!

Willy   I'm definitely going to get one. Because lots of time I'm on the road, and I think to myself, what I must be missing on the radio!

Howard   Don't you have a radio in the car?

Willy   Well, yeah, but who ever thinks of turning it on?

Howard   Say, aren't you supposed to be in Boston?

Willy   That's what I want to talk to you about, Howard. You got a minute? (*He draws a chair in from the wing.*)

Howard   What happened? What're you doing here?

Willy   Well . . .

Howard   You didn't crack up again, did you?

Willy   Oh, no. No . . .

Howard   Geez, you had me worried there for a minute. What's the trouble?

Willy   Well, tell you the truth, Howard. I've come to the decision that I'd rather not travel any more.

Howard   Not travel! Well, what'll you do?

Willy   Remember, Christmas time, when you had the party here? You said you'd try to think of some spot for me here in town.

Howard   With us?

Willy   Well, sure.

Howard   Oh, yeah, yeah. I remember. Well, I couldn't think of anything for you, Willy.

Willy   I tell ya, Howard. The kids are all grown up, y'know. I don't need much any more. If I could take home – well, sixty-five dollars a week, I could swing it.

Howard   Yeah, but Willy, see I –

Willy   I tell ya why, Howard. Speaking frankly and between the two of us, y'know – I'm just a little tired.

Howard   Oh, I could understand that, Willy. But you're a road man, Willy, and we do a road business. We've only got a half-dozen salesmen on the floor here.

Willy   God knows, Howard, I never asked a favor of any man. But I was with the firm when your father used to carry you in here in his arms.

Howard   I know that, Willy, but –

Willy   Your father came to me the day you were born and asked me what I thought of the name of Howard, may he rest in peace.

Howard   I appreciate that, Willy, but there just is no spot here for you. If I had a spot I'd slam you right in, but I just don't have a single solitary spot.

He looks for his lighter. **Willy** *has picked it up and gives it to him. Pause.*

Willy (*with increasing anger*)   Howard, all I need to set my table is fifty dollars a week.

Howard   But where am I going to put you, kid?

Willy   Look, it isn't a question of whether I can sell merchandise, is it?

Howard   No, but it's a business, kid, and everybody's gotta pull his own weight.

Willy (*desperately*)   Just let me tell you a story, Howard –

Howard   'Cause you gotta admit, business is business.

Willy (*angrily*) Business is definitely business, but just listen for a minute. You don't understand this. When I was a boy – eighteen, nineteen – I was already on the road. And there was a question in my mind as to whether selling had a future for me. Because in those days I had a yearning to go to Alaska. See, there were three gold strikes in one month in Alaska, and I felt like going out. Just for the ride, you might say.

Howard (*barely interested*) Don't say.

Willy Oh, yeah, my father lived many years in Alaska. He was an adventurous man. We've got quite a little streak of self-reliance in our family. I thought I'd go out with my older brother and try to locate him, and maybe settle in the North with the old man. And I was almost decided to go, when I met a salesman in the Parker House. His name was Dave Singleman. And he was eighty-four years old, and he'd drummed merchandise in thirty-one states. And old Dave, he'd go up to his room, y'understand, put on his green velvet slippers – I'll never forget – and pick up his phone and call the buyers, and without ever leaving his room, at the age of eighty-four, he made his living. And when I saw that, I realized that selling was the greatest career a man could want. 'Cause what could be more satisfying than to be able to go, at the age of eighty-four, into twenty or thirty different cities, and pick up a phone, and be remembered and loved and helped by so many different people? Do you know? when he died – and by the way he died the death of a salesman, in his green velvet slippers in the smoker of the New York, New Haven and Hartford, going into Boston – when he died, hundreds of salesmen and buyers were at his funeral. Things were sad on a lotta trains for months after that. (*He stands up.* **Howard** *has not looked at him.*) In those days there was personality in it, Howard. There was respect, and comradeship, and gratitude in it. Today, it's all cut and dried, and there's no chance for bringing friendship to bear – or personality. You see what I mean? They don't know me any more.

Howard (*moving away, toward the right*) That's just the thing, Willy.

Willy   If I had forty dollars a week – that's all I'd need. Forty dollars, Howard.

Howard   Kid, I can't take blood from a stone, I –

Willy (*desperation is on him now*)   Howard, the year Al Smith was nominated, your father came to me and –

Howard (*starting to go off*)   I've got to see some people, kid.

Willy (*stopping him*)   I'm talking about your father! There were promises made across this desk! You mustn't tell me you've got people to see – I put thirty-four years into this firm, Howard, and now I can't pay my insurance! You can't eat the orange and throw the peel away – a man is not a piece of fruit! (*After a pause.*) Now pay attention. Your father – in 1928 I had a big year. I averaged a hundred and seventy dollars a week in commissions.

Howard (*impatiently*)   Now, Willy, you never averaged –

Willy (*banging his hand on the desk*)   I averaged a hundred and seventy dollars a week in the year of 1928! And your father came to me – or rather, I was in the office here – it was right over this desk – and he put his hand on my shoulder –

Howard (*getting up*)   You'll have to excuse me, Willy, I gotta see some people. Pull yourself together. (*Going out.*) I'll be back in a little while.

On **Howard**'s *exit, the light on his chair grows very bright and strange.*

Willy   Pull myself together! What the hell did I say to him? My God, I was yelling at him! How could I! (**Willy** *breaks off, staring at the light, which occupies the chair, animating it. He approaches this chair, standing across the desk from it.*) Frank, Frank, don't you remember what you told me that time? How you put your hand on my shoulder, and Frank . . . (*He leans on the desk and as he speaks the dead man's name he accidentally switches on the recorder, and instantly:*)

Howard's Son   ' . . . of New York is Albany. The capital of Ohio is Cincinnati, the capital of Rhode Island is . . . ' (*The recitation continues.*)

Willy (*leaping away with fright, shouting*)   Ha! Howard! Howard! Howard!

Howard (*rushing in*)   What happened?

Willy (*pointing at the machine, which continues nasally, childishly, with the capital cities*)   Shut it off! Shut it off!

Howard (*pulling the plug out*)   Look, Willy . . .

Willy (*pressing his hands to his eyes*)   I gotta get myself some coffee. I'll get some coffee . . .

Willy *starts to walk out.* **Howard** *stops him.*

Howard (*rolling up the cord*)   Willy, look . .

Willy   I'll go to Boston.

Howard   Willy, you can't go to Boston for us.

Willy   Why can't I go?

Howard   I don't want you to represent us. I've been meaning to tell you for a long time now.

Willy   Howard, are you firing me?

Howard   I think you need a good long rest, Willy.

Willy   Howard –

Howard   And when you feel better, come back, and we'll see if we can work something out.

Willy   But I gotta earn money, Howard. I'm in no position to –

Howard   Where are your sons? Why don't your sons give you a hand?

Willy   They're working on a very big deal.

Howard   This is no time for false pride, Willy. You go to your sons and you tell them that you're tired. You've got two great boys, haven't you?

Willy   Oh, no question, no question, but in the meantime . . .

Howard   Then that's that, heh?

Willy   All right, I'll go to Boston tomorrow.

Howard   No, no.

Willy   I can't throw myself on my sons. I'm not a cripple!

Howard   Look, kid, I'm busy this morning.

Willy (*grasping* **Howard**'s *arm*)   Howard, you've got to let me go to Boston!

Howard (*hard, keeping himself under control*)   I've got a line of people to see this morning. Sit down, take five minutes, and pull yourself together, and then go home, will ya? I need the office, Willy. (*He starts to go, turns, remembering the recorder, starts to push off the table holding the recorder.*) Oh, yeah. Whenever you can this week, stop by and drop off the samples. You'll feel better, Willy, and then come back and we'll talk. Pull yourself together, kid, there's people outside.

Howard *exits, pushing the table off left.* **Willy** *stares into space, exhausted. Now the music is heard –* **Ben**'s *music – first distantly, then closer, closer. As* **Willy** *speaks,* **Ben** *enters from the right. He carries valise and umbrella.*

Willy   Oh, Ben, how did you do it? What is the answer? Did you wind up the Alaska deal already?

Ben   Doesn't take much time if you know what you're doing. Just a short business trip. Boarding ship in an hour. Wanted to say good-bye.

Willy   Ben, I've got to talk to you.

Ben (*glancing at his watch*)   Haven't the time, William.

Willy (*crossing the apron to* **Ben**)   Ben, nothing's working out. I don't know what to do.

Ben   Now, look here, William. I've bought timberland in Alaska and I need a man to look after things for me.

Willy   God, timberland! Me and my boys in those grand outdoors!

Ben   You've a new continent at your doorstep, William. Get out of these cities, they're full of talk and time payments and courts of law. Screw on your fists and you can fight for a fortune up there.

Willy   Yes, yes! Linda, Linda!

Linda *enters as of old, with the wash.*

Linda   Oh, you're back?

Ben   I haven't much time.

Willy   No, wait! Linda, he's got a proposition for me in Alaska.

Linda   But you've got – (*To* **Ben**.) He's got a beautiful job here.

Willy   But in Alaska, kid, I could –

Linda   You're doing well enough, Willy!

Ben (*to* **Linda**)   Enough for what, my dear?

Linda (*frightened of* **Ben** *and angry at him*)   Don't say those things to him! Enough to be happy right here, right now. (*To* **Willy**, *while* **Ben** *laughs*.) Why must everybody conquer the world? You're well liked, and the boys love you, and someday – (*To* **Ben**.) Why, old man Wagner told him just the other day that if he keeps it up he'll be a member of the firm, didn't he, Willy?

Willy   Sure, sure. I am building something with this firm, Ben, and if a man is building something he must be on the right track, mustn't he?

Ben   What are you building? Lay your hand on it. Where is it?

Willy (*hesitantly*)   That's true, Linda, there's nothing.

Linda   Why? (*To* **Ben**.) There's a man eighty-four years old –

Willy   That's right, Ben, that's right. When I look at that man I say, what is there to worry about?

Ben Bah!

Willy It's true, Ben. All he has to do is go into any city, pick up the phone, and he's making his living and you know why?

Ben (*picking up his valise*)   I've got to go.

Willy (*holding **Ben** back*)   Look at this boy!

Biff, *in his high school sweater, enters carrying suitcase.* **Happy** *carries* **Biff**'s *shoulder guards, gold helmet, and football pants.*

Willy Without a penny to his name, three great universities are begging for him, and from there the sky's the limit, because it's not what you do, Ben. It's who you know and the smile on your face! It's contacts, Ben, contacts! The whole wealth of Alaska passes over the lunch table at the Commodore Hotel, and that's the wonder, the wonder of this country, that a man can end with diamonds here on the basis of being liked! (*He turns to **Biff**.*) And that's why when you get out on that field today it's important. Because thousands of people will be rooting for you and loving you. (*To **Ben**, who has again begun to leave.*) And Ben! when he walks into a business office his name will sound out like a bell and all the doors will open to him! I've seen it, Ben, I've seen it a thousand times! You can't feel it with your hand like timber, but it's there!

Ben Good-bye, William.

Willy Ben, am I right? Don't you think I'm right? I value your advice.

Ben There's a new continent at your doorstep, William. You could walk out rich. Rich! (*He is gone.*)

Willy We'll do it here, Ben! You hear me? We're gonna do it here!

*Young **Bernard** rushes in. The gay music of the boys is heard.*

Bernard Oh, gee, I was afraid you left already!

Willy Why? What time is it?

Bernard It's half-past one!

Willy   Well, come on, everybody! Ebbets Field next stop! Where's the pennants? (*He rushes through the wall-line of the kitchen and out into the living-room.*)

Linda (*to* **Biff**)   Did you pack fresh underwear?

Biff (*who has been limbering up*)   I want to go!

Bernard   Biff, I'm carrying your helmet, ain't I?

Happy   No, I'm carrying the helmet.

Bernard   Oh, Biff, you promised me.

Happy   I'm carrying the helmet.

Bernard   How am I going to get in the locker room?

Linda   Let him carry the shoulder guards. (*She puts her coat and hat on in the kitchen.*)

Bernard   Can I, Biff? 'Cause I told everybody I'm going to be in the locker room.

Happy   In Ebbets Field it's the clubhouse.

Bernard   I meant the clubhouse. Biff!

Happy   Biff!

Biff (*grandly, after a slight pause*)   Let him carry the shoulder guards.

Happy (*as he gives* **Bernard** *the shoulder guards*)   Stay close to us now.

Willy *rushes in with the pennants.*

Willy (*handing them out*)   Everybody wave when Biff comes out on the field. (**Happy** and **Bernard** *run off.*) You set now, boy?

The music has died away.

Biff   Ready to go, Pop. Every muscle is ready.

Willy (*at the edge of the apron*)   You realize what this means?

Biff   That's right, Pop.

Willy (*feeling* **Biff**'*s muscles*)   You're comin' home this afternoon captain of the All-Scholastic Championship Team of the City of New York.

Biff   I got it, Pop. And remember, pal, when I take off my helmet, that touchdown is for you.

Willy   Let's go! (*He is starting out, with his arm around* **Biff**, *when* **Charley** *enters, as of old, in knickers.*) I got no room for you, Charley.

Charley   Room? For what?

Willy   In the car.

Charley   You goin' for a ride? I wanted to shoot some casino.

Willy (*furiously*)   Casino! (*Incredulously.*) Don't you realize what today is?

Linda   Oh, he knows, Willy. He's just kidding you.

Willy   That's nothing to kid about!

Charley   No, Linda, what's goin' on?

Linda   He's playing in Ebbets Field.

Charley   Baseball in this weather?

Willy   Don't talk to him. Come on, come on! (*He is pushing them out.*)

Charley   Wait a minute, didn't you hear the news?

Willy   What?

Charley   Don't you listen to the radio? Ebbets Field just blew up.

Willy   You go to hell! (**Charley** *laughs. Pushing them out:*) Come on, come on! We're late.

Charley (*as they go*)   Knock a homer, Biff, knock a homer!

Willy (*the last to leave, turning to* **Charley**)   I don't think that was funny, Charley. This is the greatest day of his life.

Charley   Willy, when are you going to grow up?

Willy   Yeah, heh? When this game is over, Charley, you'll be laughing out of the other side of your face. They'll be calling him another Red Grange. Twenty-five thousand a year.

Charley (*kidding*)   Is that so?

Willy   Yeah, that's so.

Charley   Well, then, I'm sorry, Willy. But tell me something.

Willy   What?

Charley   Who is Red Grange?

Willy   Put up your hands. Goddam you, put up your hands!

Charley, *chuckling, shakes his head and walks away, around the left corner of the stage.* **Willy** *follows him. The music rises to a mocking frenzy.*

Willy   Who the hell do you think you are, better than everybody else? You don't know everything, you big, ignorant, stupid . . . Put up your hands!

Light rises, on the right side of the forestage, on a small table in the reception room of **Charley**'s *office. Traffic sounds are heard.* **Bernard**, *now mature, sits whistling to himself. A pair of tennis rackets and an overnight bag are on the floor beside him.*

Willy (*offstage*)   What are you walking away for? Don't walk away! If you're going to say something say it to my face! I know you laugh at me behind my back. You'll laugh out of the other side of your goddam face after this game. Touchdown! Touchdown! Eighty thousand people! Touchdown! Right between the goal posts.

Bernard *is a quiet, earnest, but self-assured young man.*

Willy's *voice is coming from right upstage now.* **Bernard** *lowers his feet off the table and listens.* **Jenny**, *his father's secretary, enters.*

Jenny (*distressed*)   Say, Bernard, will you go out in the hall?

Bernard   What is that noise? Who is it?

Jenny   Mr Loman. He just got off the elevator.

Bernard (*getting up*)   Who's he arguing with?

Jenny   Nobody. There's nobody with him. I can't deal with him any more, and your father gets all upset every time he comes. I've got a lot of typing to do, and your father's waiting to sign it. Will you see him?

Willy (*entering*)   Touchdown! Touch – (*He sees* **Jenny**.) Jenny, Jenny, good to see you. How're ya? Workin'? Or still honest?

Jenny   Fine. How've you been feeling?

Willy   Not much any more, Jenny. Ha, ha! (*He is surprised to see the rackets.*)

Bernard   Hello, Uncle Willy.

Willy (*almost shocked*)   Bernard! Well, look who's here! (*He comes quickly, guiltily, to* **Bernard** *and warmly shakes his hand.*)

Bernard   How are you? Good to see you.

Willy   What are you doing here?

Bernard   Oh, just stopped by to see Pop. Get off my feet till my train leaves. I'm going to Washington in a few minutes.

Willy   Is he in?

Bernard   Yes, he's in his office with the accountant. Sit down.

Willy (*sitting down*)   What're you going to do in Washington?

Bernard   Oh, just a case I've got there, Willy.

Willy   That so? (*Indicating the rackets.*) You going to play tennis there?

Bernard   I'm staying with a friend who's got a court.

Willy   Don't say. His own tennis court. Must be fine people, I bet.

Bernard   They are, very nice. Dad tells me Biff's in town.

Willy (*with a big smile*)   Yeah, Biff's in. Working on a very big deal, Bernard.

Bernard   What's Biff doing?

Willy   Well, he's been doing very big things in the West. But he decided to establish himself here. Very big. We're having dinner. Did I hear your wife had a boy?

Bernard   That's right. Our second.

Willy   Two boys! What do you know!

Bernard   What kind of a deal has Biff got?

Willy   Well, Bill Oliver – very big sporting-goods man – he wants Biff very badly. Called him in from the West. Long distance, *carte blanche*, special deliveries. Your friends have their own private tennis court?

Bernard   You still with the old firm, Willy?

Willy (*after a pause*)   I'm – I'm overjoyed to see how you made the grade, Bernard, overjoyed. It's an encouraging thing to see a young man really – really – Looks very good for Biff – very – (*He breaks off, then:*) Bernard – (*He is so full of emotion, he breaks off again.*)

Bernard   What is it, Willy?

Willy (*small and alone*)   What – what's the secret?

Bernard   What secret?

Willy   How – how did you? Why didn't he ever catch on?

Bernard   I wouldn't know that, Willy.

Willy (*confidentially, desperately*)   You were his friend, his boyhood friend. There's something I don't understand about it. His life ended after that Ebbets Field game. From the age of seventeen nothing good ever happened to him.

Bernard   He never trained himself for anything.

Willy   But he did, he did. After high school he took so many correspondence courses. Radio mechanics; television; God knows what, and never made the slightest mark.

Bernard (*taking off his glasses*)   Willy, do you want to talk candidly?

Willy (*rising, faces* **Bernard**)   I regard you as a very brilliant man, Bernard. I value your advice.

Bernard   Oh, the hell with the advice, Willy. I couldn't advise you. There's just one thing I've always wanted to ask you. When he was supposed to graduate, and the math teacher flunked him –

Willy   Oh, that son-of-a-bitch ruined his life.

Bernard   Yeah, but, Willy, all he had to do was go to summer school and make up that subject.

Willy   That's right, that's right.

Bernard   Did you tell him not to go to summer school?

Willy   Me? I begged him to go. I ordered him to go!

Bernard   Then why wouldn't he go?

Willy   Why? Why! Bernard, that question has been trailing me like a ghost for the last fifteen years. He flunked the subject, and laid down and died like a hammer hit him!

Bernard   Take it easy, kid.

Willy   Let me talk to you – I got nobody to talk to. Bernard, Bernard, was it my fault? Y'see? It keeps going around in my mind, maybe I did something to him. I got nothing to give him.

Bernard   Don't take it so hard.

Willy   Why did he lay down? What is the story there? You were his friend!

Bernard   Willy, I remember, it was June, and our grades came out. And he'd flunked math.

Willy That son-of-a-bitch!

Bernard No, it wasn't right then. Biff just got very angry, I remember, and he was ready to enroll in summer school.

Willy (*surprised*) He was?

Bernard He wasn't beaten by it at all. But then, Willy, he disappeared from the block for almost a month. And I got the idea that he'd gone up to New England to see you. Did he have a talk with you then?

Willy *stares in silence.*

Bernard Willy?

Willy (*with a strong edge of resentment in his voice*) Yeah, he came to Boston. What about it?

Bernard Well, just that when he came back – I'll never forget this, it always mystifies me. Because I'd thought so well of Biff, even though he'd always taken advantage of me. I loved him, Willy, y'know? And he came back after that month and took his sneakers – remember those sneakers with 'University of Virginia' printed on them? He was so proud of those, wore them every day. And he took them down in the cellar, and burned them up in the furnace. We had a fist fight. It lasted at least half an hour. Just the two of us, punching each other down the cellar, and crying right through it. I've often thought of how strange it was that I knew he'd given up his life. What happened in Boston, Willy?

Willy *looks at him as at an intruder.*

Bernard I just bring it up because you asked me.

Willy (*angrily*) Nothing. What do you mean, 'What happened?' What's that got to do with anything?

Bernard Well, don't get sore.

Willy What are you trying to do, blame it on me? If a boy lays down is that my fault?

Bernard Now, Willy, don't get –

Willy   Well, don't – don't talk to me that way! What does that mean, 'What happened?'

Charley enters. *He is in his vest, and he carries a bottle of bourbon.*

Charley   Hey, you're going to miss that train. (*He waves the bottle.*)

Bernard   Yeah, I'm going. (*He takes the bottle.*) Thanks, Pop. (*He picks up his rackets and bag.*) Good-bye, Willy, and don't worry about it. You know, 'If at first you don't succeed . . . '

Willy   Yes, I believe in that.

Bernard   But sometimes, Willy, it's better for a man just to walk away.

Willy   Walk away?

Bernard   That's right.

Willy   But if you can't walk away?

Bernard (*after a slight pause*)   I guess that's when it's tough. (*Extending his hand.*) Good-bye, Willy.

Willy (*shaking **Bernard**'s hand*)   Good-bye, boy.

Charley (*an arm on **Bernard**'s shoulder*)   How do you like this kid? Gonna argue a case in front of the Supreme Court.

Bernard (*protesting*)   Pop!

Willy (*genuinely shocked, pained, and happy*)   No! The Supreme Court!

Bernard   I gotta run. 'By, Dad!

Charley   Knock 'em dead, Bernard!

Bernard *goes off.*

Willy (*as **Charley** takes out his wallet*)   The Supreme Court! And he didn't even mention it!

Charley (*counting out money on the desk*)   He don't have to – he's gonna do it.

Willy   And you never told him what to do, did you? You never took any interest in him.

Charley   My salvation is that I never took any interest in anything. There's some money – fifty dollars. I got an accountant inside.

Willy   Charley, look . . . (*With difficulty.*) I got my insurance to pay. If you can manage it – I need a hundred and ten dollars.

Charley *doesn't reply for a moment; merely stops moving.*

Willy   I'd draw it from my bank but Linda would know, and I . . .

Charley   Sit down, Willy.

Willy (*moving toward the chair*)   I'm keeping an account of everything, remember. I'll pay every penny back. (*He sits.*)

Charley   Now listen to me, Willy.

Willy   I want you to know I appreciate . . .

Charley (*sitting down on the table*)   Willy, what're you doin'? What the hell is goin' on in your head?

Willy   Why? I'm simply . . .

Charley   I offered you a job. You can make fifty dollars a week. And I won't send you on the road.

Willy   I've got a job.

Charley   Without pay? What kind of a job is a job without pay? (*He rises.*) Now, look, kid, enough is enough. I'm no genius but I know when I'm being insulted.

Willy   Insulted!

Charley   Why don't you want to work for me?

Willy   What's the matter with you? I've got a job.

Charley   Then what're you walkin' in here every week for?

Willy (*getting up*)   Well, if you don't want me to walk in here –

Charley   I am offering you a job.

Willy   I don't want your goddam job!

Charley   When the hell are you going to grow up?

Willy (*furiously*)   You big ignoramus, if you say that to me again I'll rap you one! I don't care how big you are! (*He's ready to fight.*)

Pause.

Charley (*kindly, going to him*)   How much do you need, Willy?

Willy   Charley, I'm strapped, I'm strapped. I don't know what to do. I was just fired.

Charley   Howard fired you?

Willy   That snotnose. Imagine that? I named him. I named him Howard.

Charley   Willy, when're you gonna realize that them things don't mean anything? You named him Howard, but you can't sell that. The only thing you got in this world is what you can sell. And the funny thing is that you're a salesman, and you don't know that.

Willy   I've always tried to think otherwise, I guess. I always felt that if a man was impressive, and well liked, that nothing –

Charley   Why must everybody like you? Who liked J.P. Morgan? Was he impressive? In a Turkish bath he'd look like a butcher. But with his pockets on he was very well liked. Now listen, Willy, I know you don't like me, and nobody can say I'm in love with you, but I'll give you a job because – just for the hell of it, put it that way. Now what do you say?

Willy   I – I just can't work for you, Charley.

Charley   What're you, jealous of me?

Willy   I can't work for you, that's all, don't ask me why.

Charley (*angered, takes out more bills*) You been jealous of me all your life, you damned fool! Here, pay your insurance. (*He puts the money in* **Willy**'s *hand*.)

Willy I'm keeping strict accounts.

Charley I've got some work to do. Take care of yourself. And pay your insurance.

Willy (*moving to the right*) Funny, y'know? After all the highways, and the trains, and the appointments, and the years, you end up worth more dead than alive.

Charley Willy, nobody's worth nothin' dead. (*After a slight pause.*) Did you hear what I said?

Willy *stands still, dreaming.*

Charley Willy!

Willy Apologize to Bernard for me when you see him. I didn't mean to argue with him. He's a fine boy. They're all fine boys, and they'll end up big – all of them. Someday they'll all play tennis together. Wish me luck, Charley. He saw Bill Oliver today.

Charley Good luck.

Willy (*on the verge of tears*) Charley, you're the only friend I got. Isn't that a remarkable thing? (*He goes out.*)

Charley Jesus!

Charley *stares after him a moment and follows. All light blacks out. Suddenly raucous music is heard, and a red glow rises behind the screen at right.* **Stanley**, *a young waiter, appears, carrying a table, followed by* **Happy**, *who is carrying two chairs.*

Stanley (*putting the table down*) That's all right, Mr Loman, I can handle it myself. (*He turns and takes the chairs from* **Happy** *and places them at the table.*)

Happy (*glancing around*) Oh, this is better.

Stanley Sure, in the front there you're in the middle of all kinds a noise. Whenever you got a party, Mr Loman, you just

tell me and I'll put you back here. Y'know, there's a lotta
people they don't like it private, because when they go out they
like to see a lotta action around them because they're sick and
tired to stay in the house by theirself. But I know you, you ain't
from Hackensack. You know what I mean?

Happy (*sitting down*)   So how's it coming, Stanley?

Stanley   Ah, it's a dog's life. I only wish during the war
they'd a took me in the Army. I coulda been dead by now.

Happy   My brother's back, Stanley.

Stanley   Oh, he come back, heh? From the Far West.

Happy   Yeah, big cattle man, my brother, so treat him right.
And my father's coming too.

Stanley   Oh, your father too!

Happy   You got a couple of nice lobsters?

Stanley   Hundred per cent, big.

Happy   I want them with the claws.

Stanley   Don't worry, I don't give you no mice. (**Happy**
laughs.) How about some wine? It'll put a head on the meal.

Happy   No. You remember, Stanley, that recipe I brought
you from overseas? With the champagne in it?

Stanley   Oh, yeah, sure. I still got it tacked up yet in the
kitchen. But that'll have to cost a buck apiece anyways.

Happy   That's all right.

Stanley   What'd you, hit a number or somethin'?

Happy   No, it's a little celebration. My brother is – I think
he pulled off a big deal today. I think we're going into business
together.

Stanley   Great! That's the best for you. Because a family
business, you know what I mean? – that's the best.

Happy   That's what I think.

Stanley   'Cause what's the difference? Somebody steals? It's in the family. Know what I mean? (*Sotto voce.*) Like this bartender here. The boss is goin' crazy what kinda leak he's got in the cash register. You put it in but it don't come out.

Happy (*raising his head*)   Sh!

Stanley   What?

Happy   You notice I wasn't lookin' right or left, was I?

Stanley   No.

Happy   And my eyes are closed.

Stanley   So what's the – ?

Happy   Strudel's comin'.

Stanley (*catching on, looks around*)   Ah, no, there's no –

He breaks off as a furred, lavishly dressed girl enters and sits at the next table. Both follow her with their eyes.

Stanley   Geez, how'd ya know?

Happy   I got radar or something. (*Staring directly at her profile.*) Oooooooo . . . Stanley.

Stanley   I think that's for you, Mr Loman.

Happy   Look at that mouth. Oh, God. And the binoculars.

Stanley   Geez, you got a life, Mr Loman.

Happy   Wait on her.

Stanley (*going to the girl's table*)   Would you like a menu, ma'am?

Girl   I'm expecting someone, but I'd like a –

Happy   Why don't you bring her – excuse me, miss, do you mind? I sell champagne, and I'd like you to try my brand. Bring her a champagne, Stanley.

Girl   That's awfully nice of you.

Happy   Don't mention it. It's all company money. (*He laughs.*)

Girl   That's a charming product to be selling, isn't it?

Happy   Oh, gets to be like everything else. Selling is selling, y'know.

Girl   I suppose.

Happy   You don't happen to sell, do you?

Girl   No, I don't sell.

Happy   Would you object to a compliment from a stranger? You ought to be on a magazine cover.

Girl (*looking at him a little archly*)   I have been.

Stanley *comes in with a glass of champagne.*

Happy   What'd I say before, Stanley? You see? She's a cover girl.

Stanley   Oh, I could see, I could see.

Happy (*to the* **Girl**)   What magazine?

Girl   Oh, a lot of them. (*She takes the drink.*) Thank you.

Happy   You know what they say in France, don't you? 'Champagne is the drink of the complexion' – Hya, Biff!

Biff *has entered and sits with* **Happy**.

Biff   Hello, kid. Sorry I'm late.

Happy   I just got here. Uh, Miss – ?

Girl   Forsythe.

Happy   Miss Forsythe, this is my brother.

Biff   Is Dad here?

Happy   His name is Biff. You might've heard of him. Great football player.

Girl   Really? What team?

Happy   Are you familiar with football?

Girl   No, I'm afraid I'm not.

Happy   Biff is quarterback with the New York Giants.

Girl   Well, that is nice, isn't it? (*She drinks.*)

Happy   Good health.

Girl   I'm happy to meet you.

Happy   That's my name. Hap. It's really Harold, but at West Point they called me Happy.

Girl (*now really impressed*)   Oh, I see. How do you do? (*She turns her profile.*)

Biff   Isn't Dad coming?

Happy   You want her?

Biff   Oh, I could never make that.

Happy   I remember the time that idea would never come into your head. Where's the old confidence, Biff?

Biff   I just saw Oliver –

Happy   Wait a minute. I've got to see that old confidence again. Do you want her? She's on call.

Biff   Oh, no. (*He turns to look at the* **Girl**.)

Happy   I'm telling you. Watch this. (*Turning to the* **Girl**.) Honey? (*She turns to him.*) Are you busy?

Girl   Well, I am . . . but I could make a phone call.

Happy   Do that, will you, honey? And see if you can get a friend. We'll be here for a while. Biff is one of the greatest football players in the country.

Girl (*standing up*)   Well, I'm certainly happy to meet you.

Happy   Come back soon.

Girl   I'll try.

Happy   Don't try, honey, try hard.

The **Girl** *exits.* **Stanley** *follows, shaking his head in bewildered admiration.*

Happy   Isn't that a shame now? A beautiful girl like that? That's why I can't get married. There's not a good woman in a thousand. New York is loaded with them, kid!

Biff   Hap, look –

Happy   I told you she was on call!

Biff (*strangely unnerved*)   Cut it out, will ya? I want to say something to you.

Happy   Did you see Oliver?

Biff   I saw him all right. Now look, I want to tell Dad a couple of things and I want you to help me.

Happy   What? Is he going to back you?

Biff   Are you crazy? You're out of your goddam head, you know that?

Happy   Why? What happened?

Biff (*breathlessly*)   I did a terrible thing today, Hap. It's been the strangest day I ever went through. I'm all numb, I swear.

Happy   You mean he wouldn't see you?

Biff   Well, I waited six hours for him, see? All day. Kept sending my name in. Even tried to date his secretary so she'd get me to him, but no soap.

Happy   Because you're not showin' the old confidence, Biff. He remembered you, didn't he?

Biff (*stopping* **Happy** *with a gesture*)   Finally, about five o'clock, he comes out. Didn't remember who I was or anything. I felt like such an idiot, Hap.

Happy   Did you tell him my Florida idea?

Biff   He walked away. I saw him for one minute. I got so mad I could've torn the walls down! How the hell did I ever get the idea I was a salesman there? I even believed myself that I'd been a salesman for him! And then he gave me one look and – I realized what a ridiculous lie my whole life has been! We've been talking in a dream for fifteen years. I was a shipping clerk.

Happy   What'd you do?

Biff (*with great tension and wonder*)   Well, he left, see. And the secretary went out. I was all alone in the waiting-room. I don't know what came over me, Hap. The next thing I know I'm in his office – paneled walls, everything. I can't explain it. I – Hap, I took his fountain pen.

Happy   Geez, did he catch you?

Biff   I ran out. I ran down all eleven flights. I ran and ran and ran.

Happy   That was an awful dumb – what'd you do that for?

Biff (*agonized*)   I don't know, I just – wanted to take something, I don't know. You gotta help me, Hap, I'm gonna tell Pop.

Happy   You crazy? What for?

Biff   Hap, he's got to understand that I'm not the man somebody lends that kind of money to. He thinks I've been spiting him all these years and it's eating him up.

Happy   That's just it. You tell him something nice.

Biff   I can't.

Happy   Say you got a lunch date with Oliver tomorrow.

Biff   So what do I do tomorrow?

Happy   You leave the house tomorrow and come back at night and say Oliver is thinking it over. And he thinks it over for a couple of weeks, and gradually it fades away and nobody's the worse.

Biff   But it'll go on forever!

Happy   Dad is never so happy as when he's looking forward to something!

Willy *enters.*

Happy   Hello, scout!

Willy   Gee, I haven't been here in years!

Stanley *has followed* **Willy** *in and sets a chair for him.* **Stanley** *starts out, but* **Happy** *stops him.*

Happy   Stanley!

Stanley *stands by, waiting for an order.*

Biff (*going to* **Willy** *with guilt, as to an invalid*)   Sit down, Pop. You want a drink?

Willy   Sure, I don't mind.

Biff   Let's get a load on.

Willy   You look worried.

Biff   N-no. (*To* **Stanley**.) Scotch all around. Make it doubles.

Stanley   Doubles, right. (*He goes.*)

Willy   You had a couple already, didn't you?

Biff   Just a couple, yeah.

Willy   Well, what happened, boy? (*Nodding affirmatively, with a smile.*) Everything go all right?

Biff (*takes a breath, then reaches out and grasps* **Willy**'s *hand*)   Pal . . . (*He is smiling bravely, and* **Willy** *is smiling too.*) I had an experience today.

Happy   Terrific, Pop.

Willy   That so? What happened?

Biff (*high, slightly alcoholic, above the earth*)   I'm going to tell you everything from first to last. It's been a strange day. (*Silence. He looks around, composes himself as best he can, but his breath keeps breaking the rhythm of his voice.*) I had to wait quite a while for him, and –

Willy   Oliver?

Biff   Yeah, Oliver. All day, as a matter of cold fact. And a lot of – instances – facts, Pop, facts about my life came back to me. Who was it, Pop? Who ever said I was a salesman with Oliver?

Willy   Well, you were.

Biff   No, Dad, I was a shipping clerk.

Willy   But you were practically –

Biff (*with determination*)   Dad, I don't know who said it first, but I was never a salesman for Bill Oliver.

Willy   What're you talking about?

Biff   Let's hold on to the facts tonight, Pop. We're not going to get anywhere bullin' around. I was a shipping clerk.

Willy (*angrily*)   All right, now listen to me –

Biff   Why don't you let me finish?

Willy   I'm not interested in stories about the past or any crap of that kind because the woods are burning, boys, you understand? There's a big blaze going on all around. I was fired today.

Biff (*shocked*)   How could you be?

Willy   I was fired, and I'm looking for a little good news to tell your mother, because the woman has waited and the woman has suffered. The gist of it is that I haven't got a story left in my head, Biff. So don't give me a lecture about facts and aspects. I am not interested. Now what've you got to say to me?

Stanley *enters with three drinks. They wait until he leaves.*

Willy   Did you see Oliver?

Biff   Jesus, Dad!

Willy   You mean you didn't go up there?

Happy   Sure he went up there.

Biff   I did. I – saw him. How could they fire you?

Willy (*on the edge of his chair*)   What kind of a welcome did he give you?

Biff   He won't even let you work on commission?

Willy   I'm out! (*Driving.*) So tell me, he gave you a warm welcome?

Happy   Sure, Pop, sure!

Biff (*driven*)   Well, it was kind of –

Willy   I was wondering if he'd remember you. (*To* **Happy**.) Imagine, man doesn't see him for ten, twelve years and gives him that kind of a welcome!

Happy   Damn right!

Biff (*trying to return to the offensive*)   Pop, look –

Willy   You know why he remembered you, don't you? Because you impressed him in those days.

Biff   Let's talk quietly and get this down to the facts, huh?

Willy (*as though* **Biff** *had been interrupting*)   Well, what happened? It's great news, Biff. Did he take you into his office or'd you talk in the waiting-room?

Biff   Well, he came in, see, and –

Willy (*with a big smile*)   What'd he say? Betcha he threw his arm around you.

Biff   Well, he kinda –

Willy   He's a fine man. (*To* **Happy**.) Very hard man to see, y'know.

Happy (*agreeing*)   Oh, I know.

Willy (*to* **Biff**)   Is that where you had the drinks?

Biff   Yeah, he gave me a couple of – no, no!

Happy (*cutting in*)   He told him my Florida idea.

Willy   Don't interrupt. (*To* **Biff**.) How'd he react to the Florida idea?

Biff   Dad, will you give me a minute to explain?

Willy   I've been waiting for you to explain since I sat down here! What happened? He took you into his office and what?

Biff   Well – I talked. And – and he listened, see.

Willy   Famous for the way he listens, y'know. What was his answer?

Biff   His answer was – (*He breaks off, suddenly angry.*) Dad, you're not letting me tell you what I want to tell you!

Willy (*accusing, angered*)   You didn't see him, did you?

Biff   I did see him!

Willy   What'd you insult him or something? You insulted him, didn't you?

Biff   Listen, will you let me out of it, will you just let me out of it!

Happy   What the hell!

Willy   Tell me what happened!

Biff (*to* **Happy**)   I can't talk to him!

A single trumpet note jars the ear. The light of green leaves stains the house, which holds the air of night and a dream. Young **Bernard** *enters and knocks on the door of the house.*

Young Bernard (*frantically*)   Mrs Loman, Mrs Loman!

Happy   Tell him what happened!

Biff (*to* **Happy**)   Shut up and leave me alone!

Willy   No, no! You had to go and flunk math!

Biff   What math? What're you talking about?

Young Bernard   Mrs Loman, Mrs Loman!

Linda *appears in the house, as of old.*

Willy (*wildly*)   Math, math, math!

Biff   Take it easy, Pop!

Young Bernard   Mrs Loman!

Willy (*furiously*)   If you hadn't flunked you'd've been set by now!

Biff   Now, look, I'm gonna tell you what happened, and you're going to listen to me.

Young Bernard   Mrs Loman!

Biff   I waited six hours –

Happy   What the hell are you saying?

Biff   I kept sending in my name but he wouldn't see me. So finally he . . . (*He continues unheard as light fades low on the restaurant.*)

Young Bernard   Biff flunked math!

Linda   No!

Young Bernard   Birnbaum flunked him! They won't graduate him.

Linda   But they have to. He's gotta go to the university. Where is he? Biff! Biff!

Young Bernard   No, he left. He went to Grand Central.

Linda   Grand – You mean he went to Boston!

Young Bernard   Is Uncle Willy in Boston?

Linda   Oh, maybe Willy can talk to the teacher. Oh, the poor, poor boy!

Light on house area snaps out.

Biff (*at the table, now audible, holding up a gold fountain pen*)   . . . so I'm washed up with Oliver, you understand? Are you listening to me?

Willy (*at a loss*)   Yeah, sure. If you hadn't flunked –

Biff   Flunked what? What're you talking about?

Willy   Don't blame everything on me! I didn't flunk math – you did! What pen?

Happy   That was awful dumb, Biff, a pen like that is worth –

Willy (*seeing the pen for the first time*)   You took Oliver's pen?

Biff (*weakening*)   Dad, I just explained it to you.

Willy   You stole Bill Oliver's fountain pen!

Biff   I didn't exactly steal it! That's just what I've been explaining to you!

Happy   He had it in his hand and just then Oliver walked in, so he got nervous and stuck it in his pocket!

Willy   My God, Biff!

Biff   I never intended to do it, Dad!

Operator's Voice   Standish Arms, good evening!

Willy (*shouting*)   I'm not in my room!

Biff (*frightened*)   Dad, what's the matter? (*He and* **Happy** *stand up.*)

Operator   Ringing Mr Loman for you!

Willy   I'm not there, stop it!

Biff (*horrified, gets down on one knee before* **Willy**)   Dad, I'll make good, I'll make good. (**Willy** *tries to get to his feet.* **Biff** *holds him down.*) Sit down now.

Willy   No, you're no good, you're no good for anything.

Biff   I am, Dad, I'll find something else, you understand? Now don't worry about anything. (*He holds up* **Willy**'*s face.*) Talk to me, Dad.

Operator   Mr Loman does not answer. Shall I page him?

Willy (*attempting to stand, as though to rush and silence the* **Operator**)   No, no, no!

Happy   He'll strike something, Pop.

Willy   No, no . . .

Biff (*desperately, standing over* **Willy**)   Pop, listen! Listen to me! I'm telling you something good. Oliver talked to his partner about the Florida idea. You listening? He – he talked to his partner, and he came to me . . . I'm going to be all right, you hear? Dad, listen to me, he said it was just a question of the amount!

Willy   Then you . . . got it?

Happy   He's gonna be terrific, Pop!

Willy (*trying to stand*)   Then you got it, haven't you? You got it! You got it!

Biff (*agonized, holds* **Willy** *down*)   No, no. Look, Pop. I'm supposed to have lunch with them tomorrow. I'm just telling you this so you'll know that I can still make an impression, Pop. And I'll make good somewhere, but I can't go tomorrow, see?

Willy   Why not? You simply –

Biff   But the pen, Pop!

Willy   You give it to him and tell him it was an oversight!

Happy   Sure, have lunch tomorrow!

Biff   I can't say that –

Willy   You were doing a crossword puzzle and accidentally used his pen!

Biff   Listen, kid, I took those balls years ago, now I walk in with his fountain pen? That clinches it, don't you see? I can't face him like that! I'll try elsewhere.

Page's Voice   Paging Mr Loman!

Willy   Don't you want to be anything?

Biff   Pop, how can I go back?

Willy   You don't want to be anything, is that what's behind it?

Biff (*now angry at* **Willy** *for not crediting his sympathy*)   Don't take it that way! You think it was easy walking into that office after what I'd done to him? A team of horses couldn't have dragged me back to Bill Oliver!

Willy   Then why'd you go?

Biff   Why did I go? Why did I go! Look at you! Look at what's become of you!

Off left, **The Woman** *laughs.*

Willy   Biff, you're going to go to that lunch tomorrow, or –

Biff   I can't go. I've got no appointment!

Happy   Biff, for . . . !

Willy   Are you spiting me?

Biff   Don't take it that way! Goddammit!

Willy (*strikes* **Biff** *and falters away from the table*)   You rotten little louse! Are you spiting me?

The Woman   Someone's at the door, Willy!

Biff   I'm no good, can't you see what I am?

Happy (*separating them*)   Hey, you're in a restaurant! Now cut it out, both of you? (*The girls enter.*) Hello, girls, sit down.

The Woman *laughs, off left.*

Miss Forsythe   I guess we might as well. This is Letta.

The Woman   Willy, are you going to wake up?

Biff (*ignoring* **Willy**)   How're ya, miss, sit down. What do you drink?

Miss Forsythe   Letta might not be able to stay long.

Letta   I gotta get up very early tomorrow. I got jury duty. I'm so excited! Were you fellows ever on a jury?

Biff   No, but I been in front of them! (*The girls laugh.*) This is my father.

Letta   Isn't he cute? Sit down with us, Pop.

Happy   Sit him down, Biff!

Biff (*going to him*)   Come on, slugger, drink us under the table. To hell with it! Come on, sit down, pal.

On **Biff***'s last insistence,* **Willy** *is about to sit.*

The Woman (*now urgently*)   Willy, are you going to answer the door!

The Woman*'s call pulls* **Willy** *back. He starts right, befuddled.*

Biff   Hey, where are you going?

Willy   Open the door.

Biff   The door?

Willy   The washroom . . . the door . . . where's the door?

Biff (*leading* **Willy** *to the left*)   Just go straight down.

Willy *moves left.*

The Woman   Willy, Willy, are you going to get up, get up, get up, get up?

Willy *exits left.*

Letta   I think it's sweet you bring your daddy along.

Miss Forsythe   Oh, he isn't really your father!

Biff (*at left, turning to her resentfully*)   Miss Forsythe, you've just seen a prince walk by. A fine, troubled prince. A hardworking, unappreciated prince. A pal, you understand? A good companion. Always for his boys.

Letta   That's so sweet.

Happy   Well, girls, what's the program? We're wasting time. Come on, Biff. Gather round. Where would you like to go?

Biff   Why don't you do something for him?

Happy   Me!

Biff   Don't you give a damn for him, Hap?

Happy   What're you talking about? I'm the one who –

Biff   I sense it, you don't give a good goddam about him. (*He takes the rolled-up hose from his pocket and puts it on the table in front of* **Happy**.) Look what I found in the cellar, for Christ's sake. How can you bear to let it go on?

Happy   Me? Who goes away? Who runs off and –

Biff   Yeah, but he doesn't mean anything to you. You could help him – I can't! Don't you understand what I'm talking about? He's going to kill himself, don't you know that?

Happy   Don't I know it! Me!

Biff   Hap, help him! Jesus . . . help him . . . Help me, help me, I can't bear to look at his face! (*Ready to weep, he hurries out, up right.*)

Happy (*starting after him*)   Where are you going?

Miss Forsythe   What's he so mad about?

Happy   Come on, girls, we'll catch up with him.

Miss Forsythe (*as* **Happy** *pushes her out*)   Say, I don't like that temper of his!

Happy   He's just a little overstrung, he'll be all right!

Willy (*off left, as* **The Woman** *laughs*)   Don't answer! Don't answer!

Letta   Don't you want to tell your father –

Happy   No, that's not my father. He's just a guy. Come on, we'll catch Biff, and, honey, we're going to paint this town! Stanley, where's the check! Hey, Stanley!

They exit. **Stanley** *looks toward left.*

Stanley (*calling to* **Happy** *indignantly*)   Mr Loman! Mr Loman!

Stanley *picks up a chair and follows them off. Knocking is heard off left.* **The Woman** *enters, laughing.* **Willy** *follows her. She is in a black slip; he is buttoning his shirt. Raw, sensuous music accompanies their speech.*

Willy   Will you stop laughing? Will you stop?

The Woman   Aren't you going to answer the door? He'll wake the whole hotel.

Willy   I'm not expecting anybody.

The Woman   Whyn't you have another drink, honey, and stop being so damn self-centered?

Willy   I'm so lonely.

The Woman   You know you ruined me, Willy? From now on, whenever you come to the office, I'll see that you go right through to the buyers. No waiting at my desk any more, Willy. You ruined me.

Willy   That's nice of you to say that.

The Woman   Gee, you are self-centered! Why so sad? You are the saddest, self-centeredest soul I ever did see-saw. (*She laughs. He kisses her.*) Come on inside, drummer boy. It's silly to be dressing in the middle of the night. (*As knocking is heard.*) Aren't you going to answer the door?

Willy   They're knocking on the wrong door.

The Woman   But I felt the knocking. And he heard us talking in here. Maybe the hotel's on fire!

Willy (*his terror rising*)   It's a mistake.

The Woman   Then tell him to go away!

Willy   There's nobody there.

The Woman   It's getting on my nerves, Willy. There's somebody standing out there and it's getting on my nerves!

Willy (*pushing her away from him*)   All right, stay in the bathroom here, and don't come out. I think there's a law in Massachusetts about it, so don't come out. It may be that new room clerk. He looked very mean. So don't come out. It's a mistake, there's no fire.

The knocking is heard again. He takes a few steps away from her, and she vanishes into the wing. The light follows him, and now he is facing **Young Biff**, *who carries a suitcase.* **Biff** *steps toward him. The music is gone.*

Biff   Why didn't you answer?

Willy   Biff! What are you doing in Boston?

Biff   Why didn't you answer? I've been knocking for five minutes, I called you on the phone –

Willy   I just heard you. I was in the bathroom and had the door shut. Did anything happen home?

Biff   Dad – I let you down.

Willy   What do you mean?

Biff   Dad . . .

Willy   Biffo, what's this about? (*Putting his arm around* **Biff**.) Come on, let's go downstairs and get you a malted.

Biff   Dad, I flunked math.

Willy   Not for the term?

Biff   The term. I haven't got enough credits to graduate.

Willy   You mean to say Bernard wouldn't give you the answers?

Biff   He did, he tried, but I only got a sixty-one.

Willy   And they wouldn't give you four points?

Biff   Birnbaum refused absolutely. I begged him, Pop, but he won't give me those points. You gotta talk to him before they close the school. Because if he saw the kind of man you are, and you just talked to him in your way, I'm sure he'd come through for me. The class came right before practice, see, and I didn't go enough. Would you talk to him? He'd like you, Pop. You know the way you could talk.

Willy   You're on. We'll drive right back.

Biff   Oh, Dad, good work! I'm sure he'll change it for you!

Willy   Go downstairs and tell the clerk I'm checkin' out. Go right down.

Biff   Yes, sir! See, the reason he hates me, Pop – one day he was late for class so I got up at the blackboard and imitated him. I crossed my eyes and talked with a lithp.

Willy (*laughing*)   You did? The kids like it?

Biff   They nearly died laughing!

Willy   Yeah? What'd you do?

Biff   The thquare root of thixthy-twee is . . . (**Willy** *bursts out laughing;* **Biff** *joins him.*) And in the middle of it he walked in!

Willy *laughs and* **The Woman** *joins in offstage.*

Willy (*without hesitation*)   Hurry downstairs and –

Biff   Somebody in there?

Willy   No, that was next door.

The Woman *laughs offstage.*

Biff   Somebody got in your bathroom!

Willy   No, it's the next room, there's a party –

The Woman (*enters, laughing. She lisps this*)   Can I come in? There's something in the bathtub, Willy, and it's moving!

Willy *looks at* **Biff**, *who is staring open-mouthed and horrified at* **The Woman**.

Willy   Ah – you better go back to your room. They must be finished painting by now. They're painting her room so I let her take a shower here. Go back, go back . . . (*He pushes her.*)

The Woman (*resisting*)   But I've got to get dressed, Willy, I can't.

Willy   Get out of here! Go back, go back . . . (*Suddenly striving for the ordinary.*) This is Miss Francis, Biff, she's a buyer. They're painting her room. Go back, Miss Francis, go back . . .

The Woman   But my clothes, I can't go out naked in the hall!

Willy (*pushing her offstage*)   Get outa here! Go back, go back!

Biff *slowly sits down on his suitcase as the argument continues offstage.*

The Woman   Where's my stockings? You promised me stockings, Willy!

Willy   I have no stockings here!

The Woman   You had two boxes of size nine sheers for me, and I want them!

Willy   Here, for God's sake, will you get out a here!

The Woman (*enters holding a box of stockings*)   I just hope there's nobody in the hall. That's all I hope. (*To* **Biff**.) Are you football or baseball?

Biff   Football.

The Woman (*angry, humiliated*)   That's me too. G'night. (*She snatches her clothes from* **Willy**, *and walks out.*)

Willy (*after a pause*)   Well, better get going. I want to get to the school first thing in the morning. Get my suits out of the closet. I'll get my valise. (**Biff** *doesn't move.*) What's the matter? (**Biff** *remains motionless, tears falling.*) She's a buyer. Buys for J.H. Simmons. She lives down the hall – they're painting. You don't imagine – (*He breaks off. After a pause.*) Now listen, pal, she's just a buyer. She sees merchandise in her room and they have to keep it looking just so . . . (*Pause. Assuming command.*) All right, get my suits. (**Biff** *doesn't move.*) Now stop crying and do as I say. I gave you an order. Biff, I gave you an order! Is that what you do when I give you an order? How dare you cry! (*Putting his arm around* **Biff**.) Now look, Biff, when you grow up you'll understand about these things. You mustn't – you mustn't overemphasize a thing like this. I'll see Birnbaum first thing in the morning.

Biff   Never mind.

Willy (*getting down beside* **Biff**)   Never mind! He's going to give you those points. I'll see to it.

Biff   He wouldn't listen to you.

Willy   He certainly will listen to me. You need those points for the U of Virginia.

Biff   I'm not going there.

Willy   Heh? If I can't get him to change that mark you'll make it up in summer school. You've got all summer to –

Biff (*his weeping breaking from him*)   Dad . . .

Willy (*infected by it*)   Oh, my boy . . .

Biff   Dad . . .

Willy   She's nothing to me, Biff. I was lonely, I was terribly lonely.

Biff   You – you gave her Mama's stockings! (*His tears break through and he rises to go.*)

Willy (*grabbing for* **Biff**)   I gave you an order!

Biff   Don't touch me, you – liar!

Willy   Apologize for that!

Biff   You fake! You phony little fake! You fake! (*Overcome, he turns quickly and weeping fully goes out with his suitcase.* **Willy** *is left on the floor on his knees.*)

Willy   I gave you an order! Biff, come back here or I'll beat you! Come back here! I'll whip you!

Stanley *comes quickly in from the right and stands in front of* **Willy**.

Willy (*shouts at* **Stanley**)   I gave you an order . . .

Stanley   Hey, let's pick it up, pick it up, Mr Loman. (*He helps* **Willy** *to his feet.*) Your boys left with the chippies. They said they'll see you home.

A second waiter watches some distance away.

Willy   But we were supposed to have dinner together.

Music is heard, **Willy***'s theme.*

Stanley   Can you make it?

Willy   I'll – sure, I can make it. (*Suddenly concerned about his clothes.*) Do I – I look all right?

Stanley   Sure, you look all right. (*He flicks a speck off* **Willy***'s lapel.*)

Willy   Here – here's a dollar.

Stanley   Oh, your son paid me. It's all right.

Willy (*putting it in* **Stanley***'s hand*)   No, take it. You're a good boy.

Stanley   Oh, no, you don't have to . . .

Willy   Here – here's some more, I don't need it any more. (*After a slight pause.*) Tell me – is there a seed store in the neighborhood?

Stanley   Seeds? You mean like to plant?

As **Willy** *turns,* **Stanley** *slips the money back into his jacket pocket.*

Willy   Yes. Carrots, peas . . .

Stanley   Well, there's hardware stores on Sixth Avenue, but it may be too late now.

Willy (*anxiously*)   Oh, I'd better hurry. I've got to get some seeds. (*He starts off to the right.*) I've got to get some seeds, right away. Nothing's planted. I don't have a thing in the ground.

Willy *hurries out as the light goes down.* **Stanley** *moves over to the right after him, watches him off. The other waiter has been staring at* **Willy***.*

Stanley (*to the waiter*)   Well, whatta you looking at?

The waiter picks up the chairs and moves off right. **Stanley** *takes the table and follows him. The light fades on this area. There is a long pause,* *the sound of the flute coming over. The light gradually rises on the kitchen, which is empty.* **Happy** *appears at the door of the house, followed by* **Biff**. **Happy** *is carrying a large bunch of long-stemmed roses. He enters the kitchen, looks around for* **Linda**. *Not seeing her, he turns to* **Biff**, *who is just outside the house door, and makes a gesture with his hands, indicating 'Not here, I guess.' He looks into the living-room and freezes. Inside,* **Linda**, *unseen, is seated,* **Willy**'s *coat on her lap. She rises ominously and quietly and moves toward* **Happy**, *who backs up into the kitchen, afraid.*

Happy   Hey, what're you doing up? (**Linda** *says nothing but moves toward him implacably.*) Where's Pop? (*He keeps backing to the right, and now* **Linda** *is in full view in the doorway to the living-room.*) Is he sleeping?

Linda   Where were you?

Happy (*trying to laugh it off*)   We met two girls, Mom, very fine types. Here, we brought you some flowers. (*Offering them to her.*) Put them in your room, Ma.

She knocks them to the floor at **Biff**'s *feet. He has now come inside and closed the door behind him. She stares at* **Biff**, *silent.*

Happy   Now what'd you do that for? Mom, I want you to have some flowers –

Linda (*cutting* **Happy** *off, violently to* **Biff**)   Don't you care whether he lives or dies?

Happy (*going to the stairs*)   Come upstairs, Biff.

Biff (*with a flare of disgust, to* **Happy**)   Go away from me! (*To* **Linda**.) What do you mean, lives or dies? Nobody's dying around here, pal.

Linda   Get out of my sight! Get out of here!

Biff   I wanna see the boss.

Linda   You're not going near him!

Biff   Where is he? (*He moves into the living-room and* **Linda** *follows.*)

Linda (*shouting after* **Biff**)   You invite him for dinner. He looks forward to it all day – (**Biff** *appears in his parents' bedroom, looks around, and exits.*) and then you desert him there. There's no stranger you'd do that to!

Happy   Why? He had a swell time with us. Listen, when I – (**Linda** *comes back into the kitchen.*) desert him I hope I don't outlive the day!

Linda   Get out of here!

Happy   Now look, Mom . . .

Linda   Did you have to go to women tonight? You and your lousy rotten whores!

Biff *re-enters the kitchen.*

Happy   Mom, all we did was follow Biff around trying to cheer him up! (*To* **Biff**.) Boy, what a night you gave me!

Linda   Get out of here, both of you, and don't come back! I don't want you tormenting him any more. Go on now, get your things together! (*To* **Biff**.) You can sleep in his apartment. (*She starts to pick up the flowers and stops herself.*) Pick up this stuff, I'm not your maid any more. Pick it up, you bum, you!

Happy *turns his back to her in refusal.* **Biff** *slowly moves over and gets down on his knees, picking up the flowers.*

Linda   You're a pair of animals! Not one, not another living soul would have had the cruelty to walk out on that man in a restaurant!

Biff (*not looking at her*)   Is that what he said?

Linda   He didn't have to say anything. He was so humiliated he nearly limped when he came in.

Happy   But, Mom, he had a great time with us –

Biff (*cutting him off violently*)   Shut up!

Without another word, **Happy** *goes upstairs.*

Linda   You! You didn't even go in to see if he was all right!

Biff (*still on the floor in front of* **Linda**, *the flowers in his hand; with self-loathing*)   No. Didn't. Didn't do a damned thing. How do you like that, heh? Left him babbling in a toilet.

Linda   You louse. You . . .

Biff   Now you hit it on the nose! (*He gets up, throws the flowers in the wastebasket.*) The scum of the earth, and you're looking at him!

Linda   Get out of here!

Biff   I gotta talk to the boss, Mom. Where is he?

Linda   You're not going near him. Get out of this house!

Biff (*with absolute assurance, determination*)   No. We're gonna have an abrupt conversation, him and me.

Linda   You're not talking to him!

Hammering is heard from outside the house, off right. **Biff** *turns toward the noise.*

Linda (*suddenly pleading*)   Will you please leave him alone?

Biff   What's he doing out there?

Linda   He's planting the garden!

Biff (*quietly*)   Now? Oh, my God!

Biff *moves outside,* **Linda** *following. The light dies down on them and comes up on the center of the apron as* **Willy** *walks into it. He is carrying a flashlight, a hoe, and a handful of seed packets. He raps the top of the hoe sharply to fix it firmly, and then moves to the left, measuring out the distance with his foot. He holds the flashlight to look at the seed packets, reading out the instructions. He is in the blue of night.*

Willy   Carrots . . . quarter-inch apart. Rows . . . one-foot rows. (*He measures out.*) One foot. (*He puts down a package and measures out.*) Beets. (*He puts down another package and measures again.*) Lettuce. (*He reads the package, puts it down.*) One foot. (*He breaks off as* **Ben** *appears at the right and moves slowly down to him.*) What a proposition, ts, ts. Terrific, terrific. 'Cause she's suffered, Ben, the woman has suffered. You understand me?

A man can't go out the way he came in, Ben, a man has got to add up to something. You can't, you can't – (**Ben** *moves toward him as though to interrupt.*) You gotta consider, now. Don't answer so quick. Remember, it's a guaranteed twenty-thousand-dollar proposition. Now look, Ben, I want you to go through the ins and outs of this thing with me. I've got nobody to talk to, Ben, and the woman has suffered, you hear me?

Ben (*standing still, considering*)   What's the proposition?

Willy   It's twenty thousand dollars on the barrelhead. Guaranteed, gilt-edged, you understand?

Ben   You don't want to make a fool of yourself. They might not honor the policy.

Willy   How can they dare refuse? Didn't I work like a coolie to meet every premium on the nose? And now they don't pay off! Impossible!

Ben   It's called a cowardly thing, William.

Willy   Why? Does it take more guts to stand here the rest of my life ringing up a zero?

Ben (*yielding*)   That's a point, William. (*He moves, thinking, turns.*) And twenty thousand – that *is* something one can feel with the hand, it is there.

Willy (*now assured, with rising power*)   Oh, Ben, that's the whole beauty of it! I see it like a diamond, shining in the dark, hard and rough, that I can pick up and touch in my hand. Not like – like an appointment! This would not be another damned-fool appointment, Ben, and it changes all the aspects. Because he thinks I'm nothing, see, and so he spites me. But the funeral – (*Straightening up.*) Ben, that funeral will be massive! They'll come from Maine, Massachusetts, Vermont, New Hampshire! All the old-timers with the strange license plates – that boy will be thunder-struck, Ben, because he never realized – I am known! Rhode Island, New York, New Jersey – I am known, Ben, and he'll see it with his eyes once and for all. He'll see what I am, Ben! He's in for a shock, that boy!

Ben (*coming down to the edge of the garden*)   He'll call you a coward.

Willy (*suddenly fearful*)   No, that would be terrible.

Ben   Yes. And a damned fool.

Willy   No, no, he mustn't, I won't have that! (*He is broken and desperate.*)

Ben   He'll hate you, William.

The gay music of the boys is heard.

Willy   Oh, Ben, how do we get back to all the great times? Used to be so full of light, and comradeship, the sleigh-riding in winter, and the ruddiness on his cheeks. And always some kind of good news coming up, always something nice coming up ahead. And never even let me carry the valises in the house, and simonizing, simonizing that little red car! Why, why can't I give him something and not have him hate me?

Ben   Let me think about it. (*He glances at his watch.*) I still have a little time. Remarkable proposition, but you've got to be sure you're not making a fool of yourself.

Ben *drifts out upstage and goes out of sight.* **Biff** *comes down from the left.*

Willy (*suddenly conscious of* **Biff**, *turns and looks up at him, then begins picking up the packages of seeds in confusion*)   Where the hell is that seed? (*Indignantly.*) You can't see nothing out here! They boxed in the whole goddam neighborhood!

Biff   There are people all around here. Don't you realize that?

Willy   I'm busy. Don't bother me.

Biff (*taking the hoe from* **Willy**)   I'm saying good-bye to you, Pop. (**Willy** *looks at him, silent, unable to move.*) I'm not coming back any more.

Willy   You're not going to see Oliver tomorrow?

Biff   I've got no appointment, Dad.

Willy   He put his arm around you, and you've got no appointment?

Biff   Pop, get this now, will you? Every time I've left it's been a fight that sent me out of here. Today I realized something about myself and I tried to explain it to you and I – I think I'm just not smart enough to make any sense out of it for you. To hell with whose fault it is or anything like that. (*He takes* **Willy**'*s arm.*) Let's just wrap it up, heh? Come on in, we'll tell Mom. (*He gently tries to pull* **Willy** *to left.*)

Willy (*frozen, immobile, with guilt in his voice*)   No, I don't want to see her.

Biff   Come on! (*He pulls again, and* **Willy** *tries to pull away.*)

Willy (*highly nervous*)   No, no, I don't want to see her.

Biff (*tries to look into* **Willy**'*s face, as if to find the answer there*) Why don't you want to see her?

Willy (*more harshly now*)   Don't bother me, will you?

Biff   What do you mean, you don't want to see her? You don't want them calling you yellow, do you? This isn't your fault; it's me, I'm a bum. Now come inside! (**Willy** *strains to get away.*) Did you hear what I said to you?

Willy *pulls away and quickly goes by himself into the house.* **Biff** *follows.*

Linda (*to* **Willy**)   Did you plant, dear?

Biff (*at the door, to* **Linda**)   All right, we had it out. I'm going and I'm not writing any more.

Linda (*going to* **Willy** *in the kitchen*)   I think that's the best way, dear. 'Cause there's no use drawing it out, you'll just never get along.

Willy *doesn't respond.*

Biff   People ask where I am and what I'm doing, you don't know, and you don't care. That way it'll be off your mind and you can start brightening up again. All right? That clears it, doesn't it? (**Willy** *is silent, and* **Biff** *goes to him.*) You gonna wish me luck, scout? (*He extends his hand.*) What do you say?

Linda   Shake his hand, Willy.

Willy (*turning to her, seething with hurt*)   There's no necessity to mention the pen at all, y'know.

Biff (*gently*)   I've got no appointment, Dad.

Willy (*erupting fiercely*)   He put his arm around . . . ?

Biff   Dad, you're never going to see what I am, so what's the use of arguing? If I strike oil I'll send you a check. Meantime forget I'm alive.

Willy (*to* **Linda**)   Spite, see?

Biff   Shake hands, Dad.

Willy   Not my hand.

Biff   I was hoping not to go this way.

Willy   Well, this is the way you're going. Good-bye.

Biff *looks at him a moment, then turns sharply and goes to the stairs.*

Willy (*stops him with*)   May you rot in hell if you leave this house!

Biff (*turning*)   Exactly what is it that you want from me?

Willy   I want you to know, on the train, in the mountains, in the valleys, wherever you go, that you cut down your life for spite!

Biff   No, no.

Willy   Spite, spite, is the word of your undoing! And when you're down and out, remember what did it. When you're rotting somewhere beside the railroad tracks, remember, and don't you dare blame it on me!

Biff   I'm not blaming it on you!

Willy   I won't take the rap for this, you hear?

Happy *comes down the stairs and stands on the bottom step, watching.*

Biff   That's just what I'm telling you!

Willy (*sinking into a chair at the table, with full accusation*)   You're trying to put a knife in me – don't think I don't know what you're doing!

Biff   All right, phony! Then let's lay it on the line. (*He whips the rubber tube out of his pocket and puts it on the table.*)

Happy   You crazy –

Linda   Biff! (*She moves to grab the hose, but* **Biff** *holds it down with his hand.*)

Biff   Leave it there! Don't move it!!

Willy (*not looking at it*)   What is that?

Biff   You know goddam well what that is.

Willy (*caged, wanting to escape*)   I never saw that.

Biff   You saw it. The mice didn't bring it into the cellar! What is this supposed to do, make a hero out of you? This supposed to make me sorry for you?

Willy   Never heard of it.

Biff   There'll be no pity for you, you hear it? No pity!

Willy (*to* **Linda**)   You hear the spite!

Biff   No, you're going to hear the truth – what you are and what I am!

Linda   Stop it!

Willy   Spite!

Happy (*coming down toward* **Biff**)   You cut it now!

Biff (*to* **Happy**)   The man don't know who we are! The man is gonna know! (*To* **Willy**.) We never told the truth for ten minutes in this house!

Happy   We always told the truth!

Biff (*turning on him*)   You big blow, are you the assistant buyer? You're one of the two assistants to the assistant, aren't you?

Happy   Well, I'm practically –

Biff   You're practically full of it! We all are! And I'm through with it. (*To* **Willy**.) Now hear this, Willy, this is me.

Willy   I know you!

Biff   You know why I had no address for three months? I stole a suit in Kansas City and I was in jail. (*To* **Linda**, *who is sobbing.*) Stop crying. I'm through with it.

Linda *turns away from them, her hands covering her face.*

Willy   I suppose that's my fault!

Biff   I stole myself out of every good job since high school!

Willy   And whose fault is that?

Biff   And I never got anywhere because you blew me so full of hot air I could never stand taking orders from anybody! That's whose fault it is!

Willy   I hear that!

Linda   Don't, Biff!

Biff   It's goddam time you heard that! I had to be boss big shot in two weeks, and I'm through with it!

Willy   Then hang yourself! For spite, hang yourself!

Biff   No! Nobody's hanging himself, Willy! I ran down eleven flights with a pen in my hand today. And suddenly I stopped, you hear me? And in the middle of that office building, do you hear this? I stopped in the middle of that building and I saw the sky. I saw the things that I love in this world. The work and the food and time to sit and smoke. And I looked at the pen and said to myself, what the hell am I grabbing this for? Why am I trying to become what I don't want to be? What am I doing in an office, making a contemptuous, begging fool of myself, when all I want is out there, waiting for me the minute

I say I know who I am! Why can't I say that, Willy? (*He tries to make* **Willy** *face him, but* **Willy** *pulls away and moves to the left.*)

Willy (*with hatred, threateningly*) The door of your life is wide open!

Biff Pop! I'm a dime a dozen, and so are you!

Willy (*turning on him now in an uncontrolled outburst*) I am not a dime a dozen! I am Willy Loman, and you are Biff Loman!

Biff *starts for* **Willy**, *but is blocked by* **Happy**. *In his fury,* **Biff** *seems on the verge of attacking his father.*

Biff I am not a leader of men, Willy, and neither are you. You were never anything but a hard-working drummer who landed in the ash can like all the rest of them! I'm one dollar an hour, Willy! I tried seven states and couldn't raise it. A buck an hour! Do you gather my meaning? I'm not bringing home any prizes any more, and you're going to stop waiting for me to bring them home!

Willy (*directly to* **Biff**) You vengeful, spiteful mutt!

Biff *breaks from* **Happy**. **Willy**, *in fright, starts up the stairs.* **Biff** *grabs him.*

Biff (*at the peak of his fury*) Pop, I'm nothing! I'm nothing, Pop. Can't you understand that? There's no spite in it any more. I'm just what I am, that's all.

Biff'*s fury has spent itself, and he breaks down. sobbing, holding on to* **Willy**, *who dumbly fumbles for* **Biff**'*s face.*

Willy (*astonished*) What're you doing? What're you doing? (*To* **Linda**.) Why is he crying?

Biff (*crying, broken*) Will you let me go, for Christ's sake? Will you take that phony dream and burn it before something happens? (*Struggling to contain himself, he pulls away and moves to the stairs.*) I'll go in the morning. Put him – put him to bed. (*Exhausted,* **Biff** *moves up the stairs to his room.*)

Willy (*after a long pause, astonished, elevated*) Isn't that – isn't that remarkable? Biff – he likes me!

Linda   He loves you, Willy!

Happy (*deeply moved*)   Always did, Pop.

Willy   Oh, Biff! (*Staring wildly.*) He cried! Cried to me. (*He is choking with his love, and now cries out his promise.*) That boy, that boy is going to be magnificent!

Ben *appears in the light just outside the kitchen.*

Ben   Yes, outstanding, with twenty thousand behind him.

Linda (*sensing the racing of his mind, fearfully, carefully*)   Now come to bed, Willy. It's all settled now.

Willy (*finding it difficult not to rush out of the house*)   Yes, we'll sleep. Come on. Go to sleep, Hap.

Ben   And it does take a great kind of a man to crack the jungle.

In accents of dread, **Ben**'s *idyllic music starts up.*

Happy (*his arm around* **Linda**)   I'm getting married, Pop, don't forget it. I'm changing everything. I'm gonna run that department before the year is up. You'll see, Mom. (*He kisses her.*)

Ben   The jungle is dark but full of diamonds, Willy.

Willy *turns, moves, listening to* **Ben**.

Linda   Be good. You're both good boys, just act that way, that's all.

Happy   'Night, Pop. (*He goes upstairs.*)

Linda (*to* **Willy**)   Come, dear.

Ben (*with greater force*)   One must go in to fetch a diamond out.

Willy (*to* **Linda**, *as he moves slowly along the edge of the kitchen, toward the door*)   I just want to get settled down, Linda. Let me sit alone for a little.

Linda (*almost uttering her fear*)   I want you upstairs.

Willy (*taking her in his arms*)   In a few minutes, Linda. I couldn't sleep right now. Go on, you look awful tired. (*He kisses her.*)

Ben   Not like an appointment at all. A diamond is rough and hard to the touch.

Willy   Go on now. I'll be right up.

Linda   I think this is the only way, Willy.

Willy   Sure, it's the best thing.

Ben   Best thing!

Willy   The only way. Everything is gonna be – go on, kid, get to bed. You look so tired.

Linda   Come right up.

Willy   Two minutes.

Linda *goes into the living-room, then reappears in her bedroom.* **Willy** *moves just outside the kitchen door.*

Willy   Loves me. (*Wonderingly.*) Always loved me. Isn't that a remarkable thing? Ben, he'll worship me for it!

Ben (*with promise*)   It's dark there, but full of diamonds.

Willy   Can you imagine that magnificence with twenty thousand dollars in his pocket?

Linda (*calling from her room*)   Willy! Come up!

Willy (*calling into the kitchen*)   Yes! Yes. Coming! It's very smart, you realize that, don't you, sweetheart? Even Ben sees it. I gotta go, baby. 'By! 'By! (*Going over to* **Ben**, *almost dancing.*) Imagine? When the mail comes he'll be ahead of Bernard again!

Ben   A perfect proposition all around.

Willy   Did you see how he cried to me? Oh, if I could kiss him, Ben!

Ben   Time, William, time!

Willy   Oh, Ben, I always knew one way or another we were gonna make it, Biff and I!

Ben (*looking at his watch*)   The boat. We'll be late. (*He moves slowly off into the darkness.*)

Willy (*elegiacally, turning to the house*)   Now when you kick off, boy, I want a seventy-yard boot, and get right down the field under the ball, and when you hit, hit low and hit hard, because it's important, boy. (*He swings around and faces the audience.*) There's all kinds of important people in the stands, and the first thing you know . . . (*Suddenly realizing he is alone.*) Ben! Ben, where do I . . . ? (*He makes a sudden movement of search.*) Ben, how do I . . . ?

Linda (*calling*)   Willy, you coming up?

Willy (*uttering a gasp of fear, whirling about as if to quiet her*)   Sh! (*He turns around as if to find his way; sounds, faces, voices, seem to be swarming in upon him and he flicks at them, crying:*) Sh! Sh! (*Suddenly music, faint and high, stops him. It rises in intensity, almost to an unbearable scream. He goes up and down on his toes, and rushes all around the house.*) Shhh!

Linda   Willy?

There is no answer. **Linda** *waits.* **Biff** *gets up off his bed. He is still in his clothes.* **Happy** *sits up.* **Biff** *stands listening.*

Linda (*with real fear*)   Willy, answer me! Willy!

There is the sound of a car starting and moving away at full speed.

Linda   No!

Biff (*rushing down the stairs*)   Pop!

As the car speeds off, the music crashes down in a frenzy of sound, which becomes the soft pulsation of a single cello string. **Biff** *slowly returns to his bedroom. He and* **Happy** *gravely don their jackets.* **Linda** *slowly walks out of her room. The music has developed into a dead march. The leaves of day are appearing over everything.* **Charley** *and* **Bernard**, *somberly dressed, appear and knock on the kitchen door.* **Biff** *and* **Happy** *slowly descend the stairs to the kitchen as* **Charley** *and*

Bernard *enter. All stop a moment when* **Linda**, *in clothes of mourning, bearing a little bunch of roses, comes through the draped doorway into the kitchen. She goes to* **Charley** *and takes his arm. Now all move toward the audience, through the wall-line of the kitchen. At the limit of the apron,* **Linda** *lays down the flowers, kneels, and sits back on her heels. All stare down at the grave.*

Requiem

Charley It's getting dark, Linda.

Linda *doesn't react. She stares at the grave.*

Biff How about it, Mom? Better get some rest, heh? They'll be closing the gate soon.

Linda *makes no move. Pause.*

Happy (*deeply angered*) He had no right to do that. There was no necessity for it. We would've helped him.

Charley (*grunting*) Hmmm.

Biff Come along, Mom.

Linda Why didn't anybody come?

Charley It was a very nice funeral.

Linda But where are all the people he knew? Maybe they blame him.

Charley Naa. It's a rough world, Linda. They wouldn't blame him.

Linda I can't understand it. At this time especially. First time in thirty-five years we were just about free and clear. He only needed a little salary. He was even finished with the dentist.

Charley No man only needs a little salary.

Linda I can't understand it.

Biff There were a lot of nice days. When he'd come home from a trip; or on Sundays, making the stoop; finishing the cellar; putting on the new porch; when he built the extra bathroom; and put up the garage. You know something, Charley, there's more of him in that front stoop than in all the sales he ever made.

Charley Yeah. He was a happy man with a batch of cement.

Linda He was so wonderful with his hands.

Biff He had the wrong dreams. All, all, wrong.

Happy (*almost ready to fight* **Biff**) Don't say that!

Biff He never knew who he was.

Charley (*stopping* **Happy**'s *movement and reply. To* **Biff**) Nobody dast blame this man. You don't understand: Willy was a salesman. And for a salesman, there is no rock bottom to the life. He don't put a bolt to a nut, he don't tell you the law or give you medicine. He's a man way out there in the blue, riding on a smile and a shoeshine. And when they start not smiling back – that's an earthquake. And then you get yourself a couple of spots on your hat, and you're finished. Nobody dast blame this man. A salesman is got to dream, boy. It comes with the territory.

Biff Charley, the man didn't know who he was.

Happy (*infuriated*) Don't say that!

Biff Why don't you come with me, Happy?

Happy I'm not licked that easily. I'm staying right in this city, and I'm gonna beat this racket! (*He looks at* **Biff**, *his chin set.*) The Loman Brothers!

Biff I know who I am, kid.

Happy All right, boy. I'm gonna show you and everybody else that Willy Loman did not die in vain. He had a good dream. It's the only dream you can have – to come out number-one man. He fought it out here, and this is where I'm gonna win it for him.

Biff (*with a hopeless glance at* **Happy**, *bends toward his mother*) Let's go, Mom.

Linda I'll be with you in a minute. Go on, Charley. (*He hesitates.*) I want to, just for a minute. I never had a chance to say good-bye.

Charley *moves away, followed by* **Happy**. **Biff** *remains a slight distance up and left of* **Linda**. *She sits there, summoning herself. The flute begins, not far away, playing behind her speech.*

Linda   Forgive me, dear. I can't cry. I don't know what it is, but I can't cry. I don't understand it. Why did you ever do that? Help me, Willy, I can't cry. It seems to me that you're just on another trip. I keep expecting you. Willy, dear, I can't cry. Why did you do it? I search and search and I search, and I can't understand it, Willy. I made the last payment on the house today. Today, dear. And there'll be nobody home. (*A sob rises in her throat.*) We're free and clear. (*Sobbing more fully, released.*) We're free. (**Biff** *comes slowly toward her.*) We're free . . . We're free . . .

Biff *lifts her to her feet and moves out up right with her in his arms.* **Linda** *sobs quietly.* **Bernard** *and* **Charley** *come together and follow them, followed by* **Happy**. *Only the music of the flute is left on the darkening stage as over the house the hard towers of the apartment buildings rise into sharp focus.*

Curtain.

Notes

originated in 1935.

11 *Bushwick Avenue*: a main thoroughfare in the Flatbush section of Brooklyn, New York.

13 *subway*: the New York City counterpart of the London Underground.

13 *Nebraska . . . Arizona*: the states Biff mentions here are all in the western part of the US. 'The Dakotas' is a usual way of linking two of them, North Dakota and South Dakota.

14 *counties*: each state in the US is divided into smaller geographical units known as counties.

15 *bowling*: the American version, an indoor game in which players attempt to score points by rolling a ball on a flat surface into objects called pins.

18 *chamois*: (pronounce 'shammy') leather, made from the skin of the chamois (pronounced 'shamwa') goat. It absorbs water and cleans shiny surfaces to a high gloss.

19 *Albany*: the capital of the State of New York.

19 *football:* this ball will be used for the rough-contact American game.

19 *a punching bag*: this is used for practice by professional boxers. Gene Tunney (1897–1978) was the world heavyweight champion from 1926 to 1928. He defeated the legendary Jack Dempsey twice.

20 *regulation ball*: only regulation balls, of a specific dimension and weight, could be used in a tournament game of American football.

21 *Providence*: the capital of Rhode Island; Waterbury, Connecticut, was a prosperous mill and manufacturing town at the time in which the play is set; and Bangor is a city in northern Maine. 'Mass.' is the abbreviated form for Massachusetts, with Boston as its major city. Boston is frequently referred to as 'the cradle of the Revolution' because of the Boston Tea Party (1773), one of the signal events precipitating the rebellion of the thirteen American Colonies against Britain. It was also the place where the phrase 'taxation without representation is tyranny', summarising the colonists' primary grievance, took hold.

22 *captain*: leader of a football team; a goal in this game,

called a touchdown, is worth six points; players 'pass' the ball from one to another in order to avoid a 'tackle' from the opposing team as they attempt a run to the end of the field to score.

22   *Regents*: the Regents Exams are standardised tests given in a variety of subjects to high-school students in the state of New York. Each test is in a different discipline, and a student must have a satisfactory grade in order to achieve credit from the New York State Department of Education.

22   *sneakers*: trainers.

23   *Adonises*: Adonis was a complex cult figure from Greek mythology. He had multiple roles, most of them as an annually-renewed, ever-youthful vegetation god. His name is applied to handsome young men.

26   *Hartford*: the capital of Connecticut; it is part of Willy's New England 'territory'.

27   *scrim*: a translucent theatre curtain usually made of a thin textile such as gauze. It can be used to create interesting visual effects: when light is thrown on the front of a scrim it becomes opaque, but if objects are brightly lit behind it they will become visible.

32   *shoot*: in the game of cards Charley and Willy play, they 'shoot' several rounds or hands. On the next page Willy says he's 'clean', meaning he has no cards that match (this also refers to the statement he has just made, that he has nothing to leave behind for Biff).

33   *nickel*: a five-cent coin.

34   *Brooklyn*: one of the five boroughs that make up New York City. The others are Manhattan, the Bronx, Queens and Staten Island.

35   *a pot … my build … an ace*: all terms in a game of cards. The first refers to the money that is at stake; the second to the placement of one card on an opponent's for a better chance to win; and the third is the strongest card in the pack. The game Willy and Charley like to play is called casino (see p. 40).

36   *a deck of cards with five aces*: this would be "loaded", as it should only have four.

37   *Ketchikan*: a city in south-eastern Alaska.

38   *Ohio, and Indiana, Michigan, Illinois*: northern Midwestern states.

39   *hunt*: when Willy talks to Ben about the opportunities to 'hunt' in Brooklyn, he is remembering the time long ago, before its huge population growth and eventual urbanization.

39   *knickers*: knickerbockers, men's short trousers, also known as knickerbockers, plus-twos or plus-fours in Britain.

39   *stock exchange*: the New York Stock Exchange on Wall Street is the US centre for stockbrokers and traders.

41   *yard*: garden.

49   *to take a fade*: an old-fashioned way of saying 'take unauthorised time away from work'. To do so, you need someone to 'cover' for you.

50   *Filene's . . . the Hub . . . Slattery's*: Filene's was the most famous department store in Boston in its time. Slattery's and the Hub were well-known restaurants in the same city.

50   *Spalding*: a major manufacturing company of sporting goods and related items.

51   *the Royal Palms*: a resort hotel in Florida. Its original site was in Miami.

55   *Ebbets Field*: the home of the Brooklyn Dodgers before the Major League baseball team moved to Los Angeles after the 1957 season. The stadium was demolished in 1960.

56   *Hercules*: the Roman name for Heracles who in Greek mythology was celebrated for his great strength and courage. He was the son of Zeus and the mortal Alcmena, but he later became a god in his own right as a result of his extraordinary deeds and bravery.

59   *General Electric*: most often known as G.E., a well-established home appliance conglomerate. Hastings Home Appliances is a much smaller company.

59   *Sixth Avenue*: in Manhattan, now officially called Avenue of the Americas, but inveterate New Yorkers still refer to it by its old name.

61   *wire-recording machine*: an early version of a tape recorder.

62   *The capital of Alabama . . .* : naming the capitals of every state in alphabetical order (without making any mistakes)

was a popular game American children sometimes played.

63   *Bulova watch time*: a reliable brand well-known throughout America; on radio the company advertised itself by giving the exact time of day in order to remind potential customers how accurate its instruments were designed to be.

63   *bandsaw*: a tool used in carpentry; it uses a blade consisting of a continuous band of metal with teeth along one edge.

64   *Jack Benny*: (1894–1974) one of the most accomplished radio (and later television) comedians of all time.

66   *the Parker House*: one of Boston's most elegant hotels. It is America's longest continuously operating luxury hotel and is located along the historic freedom trail on Beacon Hill.

66   *the New York, New Haven and Hartford*: the name of a train and train route stopping in several New England cities between Grand Central Station in New York and Boston's South Station.

67   *Al Smith*: Alfred Emanuel Smith, Jr. (1873–1944) was elected Governor of New York State four times. In 1928 he was the Democratic Party candidate for President, the first Roman Catholic and the first Irish-American from a major political party to seek this office. He was defeated by Herbert Hoover.

71   *shoulder guards*: part of the protective gear worn by the players of American football.

71   *the Commodore Hotel*: built as part of the terminal complex surrounding Grand Central Station on 42nd Street in New York City. It is now the Grand Hyatt.

73   *homer*: a home run in baseball that allows the player at bat to run all the bases to score a point, and also bring 'home' players on other bases to score additional points.

74   *Red Grange*: Harold Edward "Red" Grange (1903–91) was a professional American football player for the Chicago Bears.

74   *Touchdown*: a touchdown in American football, when a player catches or carries the ball across the opposing

team's end-of-field line, scores six points. There are goal
posts at each end of the field; a team scores three points
when a player kicks the ball between the posts of an
opposing team.

77   *flunked:* failed an exam.

79   *vest:* a waistcoat.

79   *the Supreme Court:* one of the three branches of
government in the United States, the highest judicial
authority in the country.

81   *J. P. Morgan:* John Pierpont Morgan (1837–1913) was the
most powerful American banker of his time.

83   *Hackensack:* a city in New Jersey across the Hudson River,
frequently disparaged by self-satisfied New Yorkers as a
reference point for all things provincial, naive and out-
of-town.

83   *buck:* a colloquialism for one US dollar.

83   *hit a number:* to win a big return on an illegal gambling
scheme.

84   *Sotto voce:* to speak quietly.

84   *Strudel:* Happy uses 'strudel', a kind of sweet pastry
usually made with apples, honey and raisins, as a
circumlocution (and a not altogether polite term) for an
enticing young woman.

86   *the New York Giants:* a professional football team. The
'quarterback' is the key player in the game.

86   *West Point:* located fifty miles north of New York City, the
prestigious United States Military Academy.

86   *She's on call:* she is a call girl, i.e. a prostitute.

87   *no soap:* an idiomatic way of saying 'this won't work'.

89   *scout:* like 'pal', another of those colloquial terms the
Lomans use with one another to express intimacy. Its use
in this context may derive from 'boy scout'.

90   *bullin' around:* used here in the same sense as the blunt
expression 'bull shit'.

93   *Grand Central:* how New Yorkers refer to Grand Central
Train Station, one of the two major railway terminals in
Manhattan (the other is Penn Station).

94   *Standish Arms:* a hotel in Boston.

100   *a malted:* a milkshake drink, very popular with New

Yorkers.

100 *a sixty-one*: Biff needs a passing grade of sixty-five points; he received only sixty-one.

102 *J.H. Simmons*: a Boston retailer.

103 *the chippies*: slang for prostitutes.

108 *gilt-edged*: a safe investment.

108 *coolie*: a highly derogatory term for a worker of Chinese or other Asian origin.

114 *a dime*: in the US a dime is a ten-cent coin.

114 *drummer*: a travelling salesman who sold goods wholesale in large lots to retailers. The term is slightly derogatory, as it implies someone who is always trying to sell you something, whether you want it or not.

114 *one dollar an hour*: a very low wage, even for the time in which the play is set.

119 *free and clear*: in a literal sense, the Lomans have paid off the thirty-five-year mortgage on their house, and now own it outright.

120 *dast*: should dare.

Questions for Further Study

1. To what extent is *Death of a Salesman* fundamentally a play about America, and to what extent is it a play whose issues reach far beyond the American experience?
2. Several important plays, ranging from Eugene O'Neill's *The Iceman Cometh* to David Mamet's *Glengarry Glen Ross*, use the character of a salesman to make a statement about America. How does Miller's play emblematise this figure as the prototypical American personality?
3. How might the scope and focus of the play have changed had Miller used one of the alternative titles under consideration, *The Inside of His Head* and *Free and Clear*?
4. How aware is Willy Loman that his situation in the play is determined by the rules of a new, post-Second World War economy?
5. To what extent is *Death of a Salesman* a play of its time and how is it relevant today?
6. How might you wish to present the play to bring out any particular aspect or refresh it for new audiences?
7. Do you think Linda Loman is partly responsible for holding her husband back from the risk-taking that might have made Willy more successful financially?
8. What might Willy have done had he had daughters instead of sons?
9. Discuss the roles Miller assigns to women as satellite figures in the play. Can Linda be considered as a character who plays a secondary part?
10. Many of the scenes in the play take place in the kitchen, yet the family never sits down to have a meal together in this domestic space. What might this say about the Loman family dynamics?
11. Why does Biff seem to be addicted to stealing? What do you think he is attempting to accomplish through this repeated transgression?

12. In the play Willy continually equates masculinity with athleticism, success in sports competitions, handling tools with authority and making an impression as a 'manly' man. What might this say about his anxiety regarding his own masculinity?

13. What is it that Willy fears about the new apartment buildings that have been constructed all around his Brooklyn neighbourhood?

14. How does Miller show the ways in which Biff's point of view impinges on his father's?

15. In the play Happy, the second son, rarely if ever speaks up for himself. Do you think his psychological situation is better or worse than Biff's?

16. What part does *Death of a Salesman* play in representing America as an automobile culture?

17. Miller dresses his stage with a number of consumer products: a vacuum cleaner, a tape recorder, a refrigerator, etc. What role do these props play as the drama unfolds?

18. Is *Death of a Salesman* tied to the multi-platform set? How would you like to present it?

19. Is *Death of a Salesman* a marriage play? What does Willy's infidelity and adultery say about the relationship Willy has with his wife?

20. Why does Charley's son succeed while Willy's sons do not? How does Charley's role as a father differ from Willy's? Consider the roles that other father figures play in the drama, including the offstage father Willy has never really known.

21. Is it significant that Uncle Ben made his fortune in Africa? What does the play imply about his ethics as a fortune hunter there?

22. What is it that Willy finds so consoling about planting seeds and working in his garden?

23. In what particular ways does *Death of a Salesman* expand our sense of how fourth-wall realism can be made to work in the theatre?

24. Music is often used as a framing device in the theatre, to establish atmosphere as the curtain rises and to extend its effect as the curtain falls. But in *Salesman* music plays a far

more integral role. Discuss the role of music in advancing the form and meaning of Miller's play.

25. Linda is the only mother figure who appears in the play. Along the way we learn that Willy and Ben's mother died long ago, and Bernard's mother, like Howard's, is not even mentioned in the play. Is this significant, or merely the result of the playwright not wanting to crowd his stage with extra characters?

26. What is the effect of the Requiem? What would the play be like without it?

ENOCH BRATER is the Kenneth T. Rowe Collegiate Professor of Dramatic Literature at the University of Michigan. He has published widely in the field of modern drama, and is an internationally renowned expert on such figures as Samuel Beckett and Arthur Miller. His recent books include *Arthur Miller: A Playwright's Life and Works*, *Arthur Miller's America: Theater and Culture in a Time of Change*, and *Arthur Miller's Global Theater: How an American Playwright is Performed on Stages around the World*.